Writing Across Culture
by Kenneth Wagner & Tony Magistrale

When I used Writing Across Culture *with my group of 19 students in Trinidad, they found it clear and stimulating. I found it invaluable—it's a major contribution to the process of intercultural learning and it should be widely used.*

—Nigel Bolland
Professor of Sociology, Colgate University

I wish every student who studies abroad brings this wonderful book along in a backpack. Students who read this book will integrate more fully into their new culture and return with more wisdom about themselves and their own society. We use the concepts contained in this book during our orientation for all our study abroad students.

—Kirsten Moritz
Director, International Programs, Brown University

As the number of students in study abroad and other types of field-based programs increases, the need for learning techniques appropriate to these situations becomes more pressing. In their excellent book, Writing Across Culture, *Wagner and Magistrale present such a tool—the analytical notebook—which encourages students to think and write as a process of cross-cultural discovery, reflection, and interpretation. One could imagine the analytical notebook being used effectively in most any study abroad or field situation where students must be equipped to cope thoughtfully with cultural differences and where faculty are looking for meaningful ways to evaluate what their students are learning.*

—Thomas Manley
Vice President, International Programs, Pitzer College, Claremont

D1432503

Writing Across Culture *performs an invaluable service for study abroad students, showing them how to turn their everyday cultural experiences into a subject of study. It is one of the very few books that we recommend to our departing students.*

—Steve Piker
Professor of Sociology, Director of Foreign Study,
Swarthmore College

I would encourage all US study abroad advisors to consider a way to incorporate Writing Across Culture *into their preparatory programming, and even to put a copy into the hands of every outbound student. The value of the book is that it empowers serious students by providing them with the tools to analyze their adjustment to an unfamiliar cultural setting, thereby helping them to understand "cross-culturally" their experiences at different points in time and in relation to their own personal growth. I believe that students who write their way through their cross-cultural experience are most likely to have the kind of profound encounter with "difference" that will lead to attitudes and acts of tolerance throughout life, and I can think of no more positive impact.*

—Geoffrey Gee
Assistant Director, International Programs, University of Pennsylvania

Writing Across Culture

PETER LANG
New York • Washington, D.C./Baltimore • San Francisco
Bern • Frankfurt am Main • Berlin • Vienna • Paris

Kenneth Wagner
& Tony Magistrale

Writing Across Culture

An Introduction to Study Abroad and the Writing Process

PETER LANG
New York • Washington, D.C./Baltimore • San Francisco
Bern • Frankfurt am Main • Berlin • Vienna • Paris

Library of Congress Cataloging-in-Publication Data

Wagner, Kenneth.
    Writing across culture: an introduction to study abroad and the writing
process / by Kenneth S. Wagner, Tony Magistrale.
        p.   cm.
    Includes bibliographical references (p.   ) and index.
1. Foreign study—Social aspects. 2. English language—composition and
exercises—Social aspects. 3. Culture shock. 4. Multicultural education.
5. Interdisciplinary approach in education. I. Magistrale, Tony. II. Title.
LB2376W26   370.19'6—dc20   95-23123
ISBN 0-8204-1923-0

Die Deutsche Bibliothek-CIP-Einheitsaufnahme

Wagner, Kenneth.
Writing across culture: an introduction to study abroad and the writing
process / by Kenneth Wagner & Tony Magistrale. - New York;
Washington, D.C./ Baltimore; San Francisco; Berlin; Bern; Frankfurt am
Main; Paris; Vienna: Lang.
    ISBN 0-8204-1923-0
NE:

Cover design by DECODE, Inc.

The paper in this book meets the guidelines for permanence and durability
of the Committee on Production Guidelines for Book Longevity of the
Council on Library Resources.

Printed in the United States of America.

DEDICATION

To our parents—Audrey & Mort, Rosalie & Sam—who have always been there for both their sons.

Table of Contents

Foreword to *Writing Across Culture*

Travel broadens the mind, we hear. Yet travel to foreign parts of the world can just as readily confirm stereotypes, misconceptions, and ethnocentric interpretations. The study abroad program, by providing an opportunity for college students to learn about a country's history, geography, language, politics, and literature, aims to ensure that participants gain an understanding of the host culture.

I have always enjoyed meeting with returned study abroad students to hear their tales from abroad. In the time since they came seeking advice while researching and planning to study abroad, they have undergone an experience that many describe as the most important in their lives. With excitement in their voices they tell of the wonders they have seen and experienced while living in a new country. Most importantly , though, study abroad advisors hear how students have changed, how different the world seems now, how the time abroad has affected the way in which they see themselves, and the family and society in which they were raised.

Study abroad, to many practitioners, is about this change. We know that while students write in their pre-departure statements that their goal is to "learn another culture," they will report when they return that they have learned most about themselves, and about what it means to be an American. What is going on? Simply put, it is that the process of "learning another culture" is at the same time one of learning that one has a culture. By comparison and contrast with a new culture, we come to see that some of the assumptions and values by which we were raised, are cultural rather than universal.

Study abroad directors, advisers, and students often discuss the process of cultural and personal discovery. But until the publication of *Writing Across Culture,* no one has written a book that explains to students how they can most effectively understand cultural differences and the consequent challenges of cultural integration. Thus, I am excited to see the technique developed by Ken Wagner, a study abroad practitioner, and Tony Magistrale, a teacher of writing. They provide students with a method—which they call an analytical notebook—in which students write about their everyday cultural experiences. This method is grounded in the "writing across the curriculum" movement which argues that writing is a mode to learning. In other words, writing about culture is an effective tool for cultural learning. Their book is the first of its kind to construct a relationship between writing and study abroad.

With this book, which teaches students how to record and study their cross-cultural observations, the issue of culture shock moves beyond the initial orientation program to become an integrated part of the study abroad curriculum. In a version of the traveler's journal extended and developed by the authors, the analytical notebook allows students to observe their own reactions and to analyze them over time. Through the record they keep in their notebooks, students can capture their own learning, and use the power of the writing process to create new understanding. Thus, the out-of-classroom experiences are not lost but become part of the educational program, to be studied as rigorously as other source materials.

Writing Across Culture takes the whole study abroad experience seriously, seeing its full breadth and depth as a rich educational opportunity. The authors document, through extensive use of student writing, how the daily brush with another culture involves more than seeing Shakespeare's birthplace or the Florentine chapel for oneself. It requires facing the difficulties of functioning as an adult, while feeling like a child, in a society where things work differently. It involves the discovery that much of what one has taken for granted throughout one's life is not universally shared. Wagner and Magistrale explain to students that it is the reaction to this reality, the shock of meeting one's own cultural specificity, that marks the core of the study abroad experience. Until this happens, our own culture remains transparent to us. Like the air we breathe, it is something we cannot see or touch or smell, yet without which we would not survive. Left unseen, unacknowledged, we are not fully aware of culture. We cannot judge it, not choose for ourselves. We are, therefore, less fully educated.

But study abroad can no more guarantee improved understanding than can tourism. Some of the tales I hear are the ones in which the storyteller's viewpoint remains unchallenged, still embedded in assumptions based on misconceptions and misinterpretations of the people and customs of the host culture. To miss the opportunity, uniquely available in study abroad, to question one's world view while in daily contact with people who construct the world differently, seems to me as sad as failing to profit from any other educational opportunity.

A few years ago, I organized a discussion evening for study abroad returnees, in which they shared in small groups their insights and feelings about cultural differences they had experienced. After spirited discussion amongst the whole group, a colleague turned to me with a warning in her eyes: "They didn't talk about what they studied." Why ever not, I wondered. At the time I was at a loss for words. With hindsight, I know what I wish I had said: "What was learned in the classroom is reflected in the grades on their transcripts. What is missing from their educational record is an opportunity to reflect on what was learned out of the classroom, in the rest of the waking hours, days, and weeks of their lives abroad.

In struggling to establish an educational credibility for study abroad, many advocates have worked hard to ensure that the classroom experience is seen as equal in academic rigor to the classes on the home campus. But the formal classroom is only one part of the curriculum abroad. A great deal of learning is happening elsewhere. As the student voices in this book illustrate, it takes place in observations, interactions, and reactions of daily living surrounded by members of the host society—as fellow students and host families, as casual acquaintances and close friends, as entertainers on television, and as actors on the political stage. And it is here, out of the instructor's view, where students try to make sense out of their own experiences. On their own, many students misinterpret their culture.

Writing Across Culture will prove valuable to students precisely because it encourages them to record and interpret their everyday cultural experiences. The analytical notebook serves as a conversation between student and teacher. The teacher is thus empowered to act as a cultural informant, gently guiding the next step, suggesting further questions to ask and stimulating further reflection. In addition, Wagner and Magistrale show students how the knowledge derived from the classroom can form the basis of better understanding of their out-of-classroom experiences.

Study abroad in all its richness cannot take its full place in an educational experience aimed at making culture less transparent and understanding more complete. Written as it is for students, *Writing Across Culture* should become an indispensable traveling companion.

Sheila Spear
Director, International Student and Scholar Services
University of Wisconsin
Madison

Introduction

This is a book about culture shock and the writing process. At this point it may not be transparent how writing and the challenge of living in a foreign culture are related. Our aim, however, is to document and analyze the connection. If culture can be broadly defined as the unwritten rules of everyday life, one effective method for learning these rules is to write about them as they are discovered. In this way, it is possible to see writing as a tool for cultural inquiry and comprehension, and hence, an antidote for culture shock. This book encourages its readers to become writers engaged in a dialogue—between themselves and their new society—about everyday cultural differences.

Writing Across Culture constitutes an unusual introduction to study abroad; it is highly appropriate as pre-departure or orientation period reading. The arguments raised between these covers were constructed by a sociologist and a writing specialist, and thus are theoretically grounded in the social sciences and composition theory. While these unique disciplines are evinced throughout this text, both authors share a similar interest in, and commitment toward, intercultural learning. And it was ultimately this connection that brought us together for this project. Our perspectives have been shaped significantly by the writing and behavior of students who have studied in The Swedish Program at Stockholm University. To them, we are immeasurably grateful. But this book would not have been possible without the help of those students in writing classes at the University of Vermont, who taught us much about the composing process. In addition, we would like to express special thanks to two former students—Jeanne Cass and Sarah Fain—for allowing us to share at length their writing with you. This book would be substantially diminished without their inimitable voices; their work is a testament to the virtues of good writing and thinking. We would be remiss not to mention that our interests in this subject have also been shaped by our own experiences abroad as students and as teachers—in Stockholm, Sweden, in Basel, Switzerland, and in Milan, Italy. The quality of our work would be diminished and its flaws all the more apparent were it not for the excellent editorial and production staff at Peter Lang: our editors, Michael Flamini and Christopher Myers; our copyeditor, Heidi Burns; and the book's production manager, Nona Reuter. We also wish to thank Linda Nathanson and Toby Fulwiler whose insights helped to shape the contents of this book. Lastly, we are grateful to Sheila Spear for her excellent foreword.

How to Use This Book

If you look carefully at the table of contents for this book, you'll notice that we designed the chapter sequence in a way that roughly reflects the study abroad experience itself. That is to say, the first chapter confronts the issue of culture shock, its emotional and behavioral characteristics, and why you are likely to experience it. Chapter two then emphasizes the central role of writing as a tool for lessening the deleterious effects of culture shock and facilitating adjustment. We are not only interested in dispensing advice and practical recommendations that have worked for other students, but also to detail the often mysterious process of how we write. Our aim is to advance a philosophy of composition rooted in the writing-across-the-curriculum movement, arguing that writing is appropriate for every academic discipline and experience, and that it is a tool for learning and self-discovery as much as it is a means for demonstrating what is already known.

The process of writing is similar to the experience of living in a new country; both activities are acts of exploration. Composing is always connected to discovery—of language, self, others, society, the world. When an author sits down to write something, she seldom knows where the language will take her, and what she will discover along the way. As an act of textual and cultural exploration, writing would appear to be a natural ally to intercultural learning. In a new society, you will need to discover cultural knowledge. You don't know rudimentary information, such as what the money is "worth," or how to ask where the bathroom is located. You don't know how to get around, mail a postcard, or perhaps, speak the language. The guidebooks will not help you solve these problems; if you are going to survive culturally, you'll have to learn how to navigate in your new society. In this book, we will help you discover how writing can help in acquiring such skills.

It is with this goal in mind that we chose to emphasize the role of the analytical notebook as perhaps the single most important writing activity available to a student studying a foreign culture. The notebook offers the ability to record information that is noteworthy to the writer; it provides the occasion to reflect upon the kaleidoscopic events that seem to unfold the moment you deplane. The notebook, as the concept suggests, is a place where students record what they think and feel about their intercultural experience and simultaneously practice their writing skills. While the intellectual goal is cultural interpretation and analysis, your writing can be informal, speculative, and expressive. But perhaps most importantly, the notebook is a place where diverse and initially unrelated observations and interpretations fuse into some kind of coherency. This is why chapter three focuses exclusively on the analytical notebook itself, detailing how to keep one, what to use it for, and why it is relevant. In chapter four, we present an entire semester's writing from one student's analytical notebook. Her example highlights the central argument of this book: that writing about everyday cultural experiences will help you to discover and understand better your new country.

Chapter five, entitled "Researching Culture," starts with the analytical notebook as a potential research tool, but goes on to consider other, more formal kinds of writing that a study abroad student may be asked to perform. As you will certainly discover soon, formal research is often an integral part of the process of cultural discovery and integration.

Writing Across Culture concludes with a final chapter discussing the connection between writing and the personal changes which typically occur to students as a result of studying and living abroad. This chapter also considers the concept of culture shock "in reverse," the experience of re-entering your own culture after living abroad.

Taken as a whole, this book essentially traces and parallels the intercultural journey as you are likely to experience it— starting with culture shock; discussing cultural adjustment, both in and out of the classroom; and concluding with a composite of what you might expect to gain from your choice to study abroad. We hope this book will make a contribution to the literature on intercultural education and that it will find its way into specific classes taught by professors who are committed to writing as a means for engaging more active student involvement in the learning process. But even if this book is not a required text, you will still benefit from reading it on your own, as it is an appropriately student-centered supplement to any study abroad curriculum.

Although most of the student voices you will encounter between these covers belong to The Swedish Program, and thus use Sweden as a representative model for discussion, we chose commentary that is universal in its applicability. The particular examples of student writing that illustrate our theoretical arguments about writing, culture shock, and cultural assimilation will certainly teach you something about Sweden. This book is not about Sweden, however. The general cultural implications and theoretical advice offered here are relevant to all study abroad students living anywhere in the world. What our students write ultimately has less to do with Sweden than with intercultural learning itself; their discussions model what young writers experience in programs around the world.

Burlington, Vermont
Stockholm, Sweden
October 1994

1

Culture Shock and the Intercultural Experience

Culture and Everyday Life

The challenge of intercultural education is to come to know a different culture. Culture, whether it be your own or that of another country, is difficult to know. It cannot be wholly understood by empirical observation; it is not a discrete object which can be seen. For example, try to explain culture by pointing to it. We cannot do so easily because culture is a conceptual abstraction: a set of ideas, norms, values, customs, traditions, symbols, and assumptions about social life.

Every society socializes its members so that we know these things without really thinking about them. Thus, individuals may not always be able to articulate their culture because such an explicit understanding is not necessary to function as a member of that society. In part, culture is taken for granted: it is the accumulation of all the unspoken aspects of everyday life. We often do not need to explain our acts, intentions, or words because their meanings are transparent, or at least they appear so to us. But imagine the difficulty of explaining why female university students in the United States need "escorts" to walk around their campuses at night to university students living elsewhere in the world where the crime rate does not intimidate people from going out alone at night. Most people simply assume that everyone shares the same social reality. This is just not true, and the extent to which you will have to make adjustments to your new culture will reflect the degree to which you will experience culture shock.

Typically, the only time most people think about culture is when they are confronted with some deviation from it. Living in a foreign country puts us in social situations where our ideas, norms, values, customs, symbols, and assumptions about everyday life are *different* from those with whom we need to communicate. Therefore, we often misread or misinterpret a given social situation.

We think we know the score as we find ourselves in familiar situations: on a date, having dinner with our host family, in the classroom, or playing a sport. Natives may act or express themselves in familiar ways so that we think we know what they mean. The problem, to put it simply, is that things are not always what they seem. The challenge of intercultural learning is to realize that "things" usually have a different *meaning* reflecting the different culture in which you are now living. In other words, things may appear to be the same, but they often mean something else.

For example, your aggressive attitude on the tennis court may seem natural to you, but to your native partner you may appear to be acting like an idiot. Your active participation in class may suggest to you that you are being an independent learner, while your classmates may think you are being a show-off. You may think that there is nothing wrong with making a cheese sandwich with ten slices of cheese (deli style), but your host family may consider the portion about right for the whole family for the week! Asking someone for a date may be no big deal to you, but the individual in question may think you are being too forward. These interpretations don't make sense? Exactly! They do not make sense to you because you are applying an American frame of reference to social realities defined by a different culture.

The problem is that most of us are unaware that our frame of reference is culturally specific; that is, it reflects the social experience of our own society. We come to assume that our frame of reference is natural, and thus, applicable to all societies. Such a frame of reference is often referred to as common sense. We think that the way we see the world is natural, "it's just common sense." But others from a different society *see and interpret* the world differently because they have their own relatively unique cultural lens. For example, Beth writes:

> I have found that I look at things with an extremely American eye. One of my first times on the subway I noticed that people could lie about where they were going (to pay less) and then ride as far as they wanted.
> When I mentioned it to my family they said they never thought about it. I think this system would be abused all the time in the States. It does not make sense.

Public transportation fares *tend* not to be abused in Sweden (and in many other countries) because there is a greater respect and concern for what is perceived to be in the public interest compared to the prevailing attitude found in the United States (Milner 1, passim). Moreover, honesty is highly valued in Swedish culture. You may be thinking that Americans are certainly honest as well. But there is a cultural difference. Americans tend to think of honesty solely in terms of interpersonal relations. For example, Americans feel moral pressure not to lie to friends and family. In contrast, many Americans do not feel guilty cheating the government. In fact, being able to "rip off the system" without getting caught is almost a form of sport in America. Thus, Beth is probably right to claim that this system would be abused in the States, but the fact that it doesn't make "sense" reflects her "American eye."

We are accustomed to using our common sense as a frame of reference which functions as an *unwritten* guide to everyday social interaction. We do not have to write it down because we know it by heart. But we often cannot use our common sense in a foreign culture. Our frame of reference is not accurate. We soon begin to realize that there is a different guide to everyday life in a new society. This discovery, however, is not enough because no one is willing or able to write it all down for you. How could something so important be unwritten? This is part of both the challenge and magic of discovering culture. You can only do it yourself. The challenge of coming to know a new culture requires that *you* be able to record your everyday discoveries and understandings on paper. It is the process of composing your *own portrait* of the culture which will eventually lead to understanding your new society.

Learning a culture, like writing a paper, requires many drafts. You must view your own initial writings on culture as sketches. You will be constantly reworking your sketches as you accumulate both new cultural experiences and meaning. In other words, it will take time to get it right, to accumulate experiences which capture the nuances, the varieties, and the contradictions which characterize all cultures. The common error is to look prematurely for a completed picture, one that is consistent and fairly straightforward. Cultural learning is not so easy. Just when you think you finally have it figured out, you will meet a native or have an experience which simply does not fit your emerging cultural composite. So, back you go to the drawing board attempting to compose a more accurate view.

This process sounds frustrating, and sometimes it is akin to the saying "one step forward, two steps back." But it is also the way in which a foreign culture is correctly understood. Remember, too, along with those frustrating moments of reevaluation, there will also be tremendous exhilaration as your perspective grows and enriches.

Cultural learning refers to understanding the dominant characteristics which describe individuals and institutions in a particular society. But we can only *witness* or observe culture through the behavior of individuals. Our observations of individuals can tell us something about how altruistic, egoistic, greedy, assertive, honest, or reserved the "people" seem to be. It is possible to compose a portrait of the typical American, or Chinese, or Italian using such adjectives. But how many Chinese or Americans or Italians are really typical? Just when it appears that you have captured the essence of a cultural portrait, something will force you to alter the canvas—to qualify your portrait by toning it down, embellishing, or redefining.

No one person embodies all the characteristics of his or her culture. As individuals we are in most ways reflections of our culture. But in important ways we are also contradictions to our own culture. The cultural tendency of visitors is to assume that everyone they meet will accurately tell us something about their new society. We are, at least initially, unable to distinguish between what is typical and idiosyncratic about the individuals we meet.

Further complicating the challenge of making accurate generalizations about "what the people are like" is the fact that there are gender differences in every culture. The behavior of individuals is mediated by how the prevailing culture has historically shaped the social roles of men and women. The problem is that you are not likley to know how gender makes a difference in the behavior of those individuals you meet or observe. It would be a mistake to assume that your frame of reference related to gender will always be a helpful guide. In your interaction with women and men, you will need to learn the extent to which their actions are a reflection of their own culture's definition of gender. This is not to imply that the men and women you meet will not share certain cultural characteristics; they will. But the social reality of gender differentiation means that they are also different. You can, of course, make similar arguments regarding the ways in which society relates differentially to individuals according to race, ethnicity, class, and religion.

How you perceive your new culture will largely depend on how this culture perceives you. A woman studying abroad in a culture where women have low social status and rigidly prescribed roles will certainly experience this society differently from a man. Your sex (as well as your race) will affect to a certain degree how the native population interacts with you. For example, how you experience the people of Australia, of Egypt, of Mexico, of Denmark, of Italy, or of any country will, in part, depend on whether you are a woman or a man (and some countries whether you are Christian or Jewish, and in most countries, whether you are a person of color).

The challenge of making generalizations must, therefore, always be qualified by a recognition that, even though all individuals in some ways reflect the dominant culture, they may also represent groups which deviate from the "mainstream."

Consequently, you will find yourself complaining that you seem to have a theory a day about "what the people are really like." When you are about to give up figuring out what "they" are really like and are tired of having your own actions or intentions being misinterpreted, you are experiencing culture shock. Shocked by the realization that you can no longer be confident in understanding everyday life, you no longer take things for granted. Every social situation requires some thought as there are no longer simple routines. You find yourself in society without the benefit of culture. Your human capacity and need to understand and communicate is threatened. You feel, in a literal sense, culturally naked. This is precisely why the term "culture shock" suggests such a dramatic experience.

You will feel shocked until you begin to develop an understanding of this *unwritten* guide to everyday life. Such social understanding, like a particular choice in clothing, gives human beings a sense of social protection against the insecurities of living in a new society "without a clue." You can begin to temper culture shock by writing your cultural experiences down on paper—in letters, in a diary, or in a journal (or using what we will later define as an analytical notebook. We will explain how to keep such a notebook in chapter three).

Culture Shock and the Mood Curve

Most students have heard of the term *culture shock*. But how many really take the term seriously? How many think that they will actually suffer from culture shock during their semester or year abroad? Our experience suggests that most students underestimate the nature of the phenomenon. Why?

Perhaps it is because most former study abroad students do not talk explicitly about their experience in ways that suggest culture shock. They know that they went through a difficult period of adjustment when they really missed home, but they are unable to describe it fully because the experience occurred several months or even years earlier, and was probably never recorded. Also, it is simply human nature to repress those moments where cultural adjustment was difficult, while emphasizing times when it occurred with grace and pleasure. This is what we tend to remember, and it is what is most often communicated to others. Before students can begin to understand and eventually articulate their culture shock, they must have a history of their experience. Photo albums are fun but they don't tell the whole story. To secure a more accurate history, the experience must be written down on paper.

The first exposure to culture shock is often felt within the first few days of orientation. Students get a sense that things are suddenly different. Moreover, unlike vacations and other previous traveling experiences, they know that this trip will be different because they are not going home soon. You may ask yourself: "Why in the hell have I done this?" You may miss home right away. Here are a few examples from students who have written about this initial feeling.

Linda, after one week in Stockholm, writes:

> Today everything Swedish began to drive me crazy, especially the language. So many "strange" sounds! Hours and hours of incomprehensible chatter! How can I stay sane? I don't think my host family understands what it's like to not be able to watch TV or talk to everyone . . . I feel so out of place and ignorant and conspicuous that I'm craving home—my family and house and yard . . . things that usually drive me a little crazy too.

Listen to Jill, who has experienced something similar:

> It's overwhelming yet in a different way than I expected. Everything even looks so different than I imagined. I had no major expectations just the usual hoping that things would be exciting, interesting, etc. Hoping perhaps to see the light or something that would put life in place. Now I'm just boggled. But that's usual in the beginning of change. I don't deal well with change. Changing circumstances frighten me. I put myself into this, though, and I have already learned a lot. I realized how set in my ways I am. Well, no! I am open to different things but have little experience with totally different people. The language is frustrating, to be surrounded by a language you can't understand. I feel stupid and young.

Jill's writing entry suggests the struggle that so often attends cultural assimilation. We listen to her from a variety of discursive perspectives: recalling her initial set of expectations, confronting her present status, and finally looking for a way to survive. In her writing we listen to her "divided voice" as her new evolving self talks back to her former, more complacent self. It is hard to imagine this apparently schizophrenic condition as a positive experience, especially when one part of Jill feels "boggled" and "frightened." But pay particular attention to the more confident voice that is slowly emerging near the end of the writing. It is this reflexive voice, the one insisting she is "open" to the challenges of her new culture, that will become stronger as she continues to learn and assimilate. You will learn much about culture in studying abroad—food, customs, language, and so forth—but the greatest learning will take place inside, as the experience slowly challenges and changes your very definition of selfhood.

The introduction of a new language significantly exacerbates the stress of culture shock. Living in a society and not being able to understand the words of other human beings around you can make you feel literally deaf and dumb. Words appear as "chatter," as sounds without apparent meaning. The important issue here is that the inability to understand what people are saying and, in turn, to communicate verbally yourself, may be the clearest and most dramatic indication that you are far from home.

Most students recover fairly quickly from the immediate feeling Jill and Linda expressed above. After the initial shock of facing a foreign society, most students become very excited about the prospect of learning a new culture. A major reason you undertook this experience, after all, was to experience the excitement of discovering something completely new.

Almost all students, however, underestimate how long it will take to feel somewhat assimilated and comfortable. The early euphoria typically comes to an end around the close of the first month. Why? In the beginning of your journey abroad new ways of thinking and living confront you as an adventure. It is fun to discover something new. Life is anything but boring. But after about a month or so of never being able to take everyday activities for granted, you begin to yearn for the familiar. Continuing to feel like a child making "stupid" mistakes becomes annoying. Things which you have always taken for granted— how to use the bank or post office, trying to find your favorite cold medicine at the drug store, what kind of food to buy or order, learning how to use a shower hose without soaking the entire bathroom, figuring out how to use washing machines that look like they are from another planet, searching for a newspaper to find out what's new in the world, or simply to finding out what place your favorite sports team currently occupies in the standings—become major obstacles. The adventure appears less exhilarating than it is exhausting.

These everyday frustrations, combined with the "simple" tasks of living, are the essences of culture shock. It is not only the abstract recognition that your new society is different in terms of values and the structure of institutions. Certainly values and politics can exacerbate your feeling that you do not "belong" in this new culture. But culture shock refers more to the simple and immediate reality that everyday life can no longer be taken for granted. Every task becomes a challenge and a source of frustration. You will begin to miss the most simple and familiar things in your life. In Andrea's words: *"it's the little things I take for granted that I miss. What gets me is: why don't they have normal salads, why don't they have chocolate chips"??*

Sarah likewise yearns for things familiar:

> The smallest things here bring out the ethnocentricity in me. I have few problems with social democracy but I find myself being critical of small and ridiculous things. The escalators annoy me.... And the juice, who wants to go to the trouble of making a drink when it is so much easier to pour something already mixed from a bottle or carton? These things seem flippant and irrelevant even to me, but it's always the little things that stand out, that point out the larger differences.

If you are reading this book before your journey abroad, we advise you not to be too critical of Andrea or Sarah. Your times of frustration will come. If you are already sitting in your room abroad, we are confident that you understand the frustration with things which seem "irrelevant."

So far we have explained theoretically why you are likely to experience some form of culture shock. We now want to make this discussion more concrete by attempting to identify the behavioral and emotional signs of this experience.

Fear and Loathing in a Foreign Land

A central emotional characteristic of culture shock is fear. One definition of fear might be that moment when you are aware that common sense and your belief in an ordered world no longer hold true. It is not overstating the point to argue that you may feel a little less human as you find yourself in the midst of a new society without the benefit of the most human of all creations—culture.

Fear, however, is often expressed in more disguised forms when one is among others. The fact that most people are reluctant to admit to feeling afraid or nervous about their new experiences is one of the main reasons for keeping an analytical notebook. Writing about your fears can be an effective way for you to face the fact that you are fearful. Fear that remains unacknowledged will surface in other ways. Here is Denise discussing her reaction to Swedish food:

> I am sick and tired of having so little choice at the salad bar at the University dining hall. I mean cut up shredded carrots and cabbage just does not cut it. It's ridiculous! Can't this country afford to make better produce available!

And Mark describes his observations of how Swedes behave on the subway:

> The homogeneous quality of the Swedes extends to their behavior as well. Those who are not sleeping or reading or listening to their Walkman are staring out the window. There is no talking or laughing or shouting.

And witness the anger underlying Bill's reaction to his first Swedish party:

> Last night my host family threw a party for my host sister's twenty-third birthday. So she invited about 20 of her friends over for dinner, and I asked two of my friends from the program. After the party, it occurred to me how few of her friends I had actually met that night. As it turns out, the reason for this is that I had failed to introduce myself to everyone. Apparently, I had been rude. Had I been to a party in the States, the host would have introduced me to everyone. Often times I have thrown a party at school and if someone there did not know all my friends, I would introduce them to him or her, usually more than once. Not so in Sweden!

The common sentiment running through the feelings of Denise, Mark, and Bill is anger. Students experiencing the full effects of culture shock often react initially by lashing out at those who make them feel inadequate: the native population. It is common in the early stages of culture shock for students to do nothing but "bash the natives" when they are among themselves. The threat leads to all sorts of expressions of internal solidarity among the newcomers; solidarity is found in sharing their hostility towards the natives.

Thus, students commonly become super "critics" of their new society and culture. Individuals who feel threatened by others often deal with their anxiety by demonizing those seen as responsible for producing these negative emotions. This reaction, of course, reflects the basic psychology that underscores all prejudice and racism.

Many students living abroad experience for the first time what it is like to be an "outsider" in society. The initial response can be harsh as we have seen expressed in the above student notebooks. The tendency to bash the natives is exacerbated by the fact that it is actually tough to meet strangers anywhere, but especially in a foreign culture. Most students begin their stay as if they were in some kind of Hollywood production; they are overly romantic about making friends, if not lovers, in a foreign land. The reality of being a foreigner in any society is that it takes time to make friends. If this seems odd or un-American, we ask you to think about the foreign students on your home campus. Have you or your friends gone out of your way to meet guest students on your own home turf? The answer is probably no. We raise the question not to make you feel guilty, for everyone has his or her own routines and busy schedule. It is very easy to walk around your new environment waiting for the natives to welcome you to their country. But making friends abroad will take time and effort on your part.

Not all students, however, who feel like outsiders become angry or engage in native bashing. We do not all respond to fear in the same manner. Some students respond by withdrawing and becoming very reserved. Others become more emotional and find themselves over-reacting to situations.

We should emphasize also here that not all students will exhibit clear signs of culture shock. Some individuals will simply repress their fear or insecurity. But most students, in some form or another, will experience varying degrees of difficulty in learning to live in a new culture. Those who indicate otherwise may not be opening themselves fully to the changes in front of them. Not allowing yourself to see or experience a new culture is one way of dealing with the fear of having to adjust to a new society. By refusing to open yourself, however, the oblivious foreigner also misses opportunities to learn from the challenges culture shock presents. So if you are aware that you are experiencing some variation of culture shock, you should at least feel good that you are open to the full range of the study abroad experience.

A more intellectual consequence of culture shock is the tendency to want to generalize too soon about your new culture. For example, after meeting two Germans or two Australians at a bar, some students will be ready to proclaim the nature of all Germans and Australians. Also common is for students living with host families to generalize about all families. Be careful! The natives you meet during the first or second week may be typical, and if so, your generalizations about the larger population may be correct. But you cannot yet be certain. You need to accumulate more cultural experiences (evidence) before you can be confident in your cultural assessments.

Comparing Cultures

The desire to generalize immediately stems from the uneasy feeling of not knowing the culture. It is more than simply wanting to know something about your new society; you *need* to know. Desperate to make sense out of this new world, generalizations promise the benefits of knowledge and experience. You will take false comfort many times thinking that you "now have it straight." Your confidence will hold until a new experience forces you to re-think past generalizations. It is important to realize that the attainment of cultural knowledge takes time.

You will also feel frustrated in forming generalizations early because you will naturally be looking for cultural consistency, assuming that each experience will be like finding a new piece of the puzzle. Such consistency is not to be found in most cultures. As stated earlier, there will be pieces of the puzzle which simply do not fit the emerging larger picture. Cultural traditions, customs, norms, and values can *be* contradictory or *appear* to be contradictory.

For example, Swedes are known for their strong commitment to social welfare, a tradition of caring for all citizens through an extensive network of social services. On the other hand, some observers in Sweden are taken aback by the apparent lack of demonstrated concern for neighbors. The apparent contradiction here is that Swedes are most generous when it comes to funding the state to care for its neighbors, but seem to be less enthusiastic about personally helping each other (Wolfe 1, passim).

A similar contradiction exists in the United States. Americans rarely demonstrate concern for the general welfare of society. Recent studies suggest that most Americans have little notion of the concept of community (Bellah 1, passim). On the other hand, Americans can be very generous when it comes to helping out the neighbors next door. It appears that, in this example at least, Sweden and the United States are culturally opposite.

Such contradictions can confuse newcomers in both societies because they make generalizations difficult. The determination of whether Swedes or Americans are socially generous and civic-minded depends on where you look. Are generalizations then impossible? No! It means that before you will be confident in your generalizations you will have to understand the nuances and variations existent in your new society. Most truths about culture are never black and white. Rather, cultural truths demand being able to see the shades of gray in most social situations. Such understanding requires both experience and theoretical knowledge.

We will discuss in greater depth the need to develop a theoretical perspective, a new paradigm or cultural lens, in subsequent chapters. For now, let us continue our discussion on why the attainment of cultural knowledge takes time.

The intellectual challenge of cultural learning is not only that early observations cannot be trusted to be typical or empirically accurate, but also that these early cultural experiences are likely to be *misinterpreted*. The problem is figuring out the social meaning of your new experiences.

This deciphering of cultural meaning is problematic because we, knowingly or not, use our "own" frame of reference (or paradigm) which is culturally specific. In other words, we use a perspective rooted in our own native culture which may not be applicable for another culture. Let's use another example. Barb writes about her initial experience in the dorms at Stockholm University:

> I was told not to expect that my floor would be like my floor in the States. But I really thought that the students on my floor were unfriendly. I mean they could have come over to me and welcomed me to my room.

Barb judges her Swedish floormates harshly because they didn't act in ways to which she was accustomed, given her experience in American college dorms. It is evident from the above passage that Barb is trying to place her experience in a Swedish perspective. It is true that in Sweden, as is the case in most European universities, the dorms are more like apartments. They are places where students simply sleep and eat. Unlike the dorms in the United States, they do not play as important a social role. Consequently, we perceive that Barb's expectations reflect an American frame of reference.

In addition, as Barb suggests, people from other countries tend to be far more shy with initial encounters. It does not *mean* that these individuals are aloof or unfriendly. Moreover, shyness in Sweden, as is the case in many other places, such as in many Asian countries, is not a pejorative trait. It is not something you have to work hard to "get over." For most Swedes and Asians, it is thought to be normal that getting to know someone takes time, and it is most appropriate to move slowly when you meet someone new.

Another good example of using your own cultural experience as a basis to judge your new cultural experiences comes from Jim. After his fourth day in Stockholm, Jim came up after class and informed his instructor that he was "getting along real well." His instructor said, "that's great but why do you say so?" Jim went on to explain, with a big grin on his face, that every time he "looked at a Swedish woman she would look him back directly in his face! After a laugh, Jim concluded, "I think they like me."

Again, we have an American male interpreting his experience with Swedish women using his own cultural past to form a conclusion. The conclusion is wrong. In Sweden, as in many other countries, women may look back if you look at them. It doesn't necessarily mean anything romantic. Rather, its specific cultural meaning suggests that Swedish women are less coy and less intimidated by male staring, a gesture which in many societies is symbolic of sexual intentions.

Another example comes from Bill who complains in his journal that his host brother is "rude." Apparently Bill's host brother never introduces him to his Swedish friends when they meet spontaneously. Bill complains:

> I am getting madder and madder at my host brother. He never introduces me to his friends. Last week, we met a friend of his on the subway and they talked as if I was not even there. How rude!

In Sweden, and in most of the Nordic countries, it is not common to introduce people in such circumstances described by Bill. It is not considered impolite. Thus, Bill's brother certainly is not intentionally trying to make Bill feel uncomfortable. Bill is uncomfortable because he finds himself in what seems to be a recognizable and clear social situation, but he does not understand the prevailing cultural norms.

So far we have used examples of different cultural customs or norms to illustrate experiences which contribute to culture shock. Let's now turn to a few examples which demonstrate how values can also reveal the colors of your own national flag. Freedom and equality are cherished values both in Sweden and in the United States. Both values, however, do not have the exact same cultural meaning in each society.

In the United States, people tend to think of freedom in terms of *freedom to act*, to express one's individual desires and needs verbally and physically. In Sweden, as in many other countries, freedom also refers to being *free from* certain conditions which are understood to limit individual freedom: to be free from poverty, crime, and economic degradation. The different meaning of freedom, of course, has clear political consequences when we look at Swedish and American public policy. But the central point for our discussion is that it can be disconcerting when you discover in class, at a cafe, or at dinner that your new friends think very differently about a concept such as freedom.

> I was at a party the other night and I got into a conversation about politics. I said that I did not think Swedes were as free as we were because they had fewer choices. This Swede really got mad. He wanted to know what choices I was referring to. I said I meant consumer choices. Then this guy said he would give up some choice as a consumer if as a citizen he were free from the kind of social conditions which imprison so many Americans. It took me a while, but we were talking about different kinds of freedom.

Such encounters make you think critically about your own values. This kind of self-evaluation shakes both the cultural and moral foundation of an individual, even if values remain essentially unchanged. It is clearly a good exercise to question what normally goes unexamined. But it is precisely this kind of personal and social analysis which fosters cultural uncertainty and produces culture shock.

Continuing this discussion on equality, we again find that there is a cultural difference in Sweden and in the States. An American child typically grows up being taught that equality means that no one is better than he or she. Swedish children commonly are told that equality means that they are not better than anyone else. Both assertions express a concern with equal status and rights. But the cultural meanings and corresponding social implications are very different. The difference is demonstrated in what is often seen as typical Swedish humility and American self-assertion.

Reflecting the political traditions of social democracy, equality is frequently equated with social solidarity which values the goals of the larger community (Heclo and Madsen, Milner, Titlon). Thus, Swedes are socialized not to stand out from the group. Attempts to differentiate the individual from others may be seen as egotism or just plain pretentiousness.

Americans are taught that equality refers more to the recognition of individual rights. And no right appears more culturally sacred than the value of individuals to assert themselves. American children tend to be socialized according to the ideology of individualism which rewards them when they are able to differentiate themselves from the group. Children are "pushed" to do better than others, and it is not socially inappropriate to call attention to your own individual achievements.

The cultural differences concerning humility and self-assertion also emerge in the classroom. Many faculty from abroad are often impressed with how willing American students are to speak out in class and express their opinion. But they are dismayed when many of these students do so in spite of not having read the material! In contrast, students from other countries are more reluctant to speak in class because they often assume that they do not know enough to have a dialogue with the professor nor do they want to "sound like they have all the answers."

There are other cultural reasons for this contrast, such as differences in pedagogical styles. For example, many professors at European universities rely more on lectures than on student participation through discussion compared to their American counterparts. We should emphasize that we think more and more professors are moving towards a classroom structure which allows for student dialogue. Nevertheless, the present pedagogical difference still holds true today in most countries around the world. Thus, most American students studying abroad will be confronted with a level of culture shock in their own classrooms.

Another cultural difference that usually emerges in the classroom is the fact that education is much less structured compared to a typical classroom in the States. For example, the syllabus is a foreign idea in many universities throughout the world. European students are given much more responsibility for choosing reading and deciding how much to read and when. Needless to say, some American students are eager to exploit a classroom situation in which the professor appears not to care how hard you work. This cultural difference is one reason why many American students, when they return home, report that their program abroad was "easy." There certainly was work to be done, but some American students simply exploit the fact that they can get away with less effort. European professors constantly express amazement as to why such bright students appear lazy in the absence of coercion from an authority figure. For example, Swedish Program language teachers have been told explicitly by their students that they must give more quizzes if they want them to do the homework. The teachers have a hard time understanding why intelligent 20 year-olds need such motivation. Their own cultural inclination is that students should be more self-motivated.

Another example of cultural differences in the classroom is student comportment. In many American classrooms, students wear baseball caps, chew gum, drink from a soda can, and perhaps, put their feet up on chairs. Such behavior may be simply thought to be relaxed and informal from an American point of view. But from the perspective of faculty and students from other countries, this behavior may be seen as rude and disrespectful. Classroom behavior in most universities throughout the world is more formal.

Becoming observant of such cultural differences is the first step toward finding an antidote to culture shock. Many early observations will be false not only because you will use your own cultural past as a guide to your present circumstances, but also as a result of becoming sensitive to culture for the first time. All of a sudden you are thinking about and looking for examples of customs, traditions, and norms. As argued earlier, you never think about such things in your own country. Why should you? Culture is the everyday world we take for granted. Knowing that assumptions are not likely to be valid in new surroundings should lead someone to become more culturally observant. The problem is that many students will make observations in settings with which they have no comparative perspective as this student did after spending only two days in Stockholm: "The Swedes are so quiet that they don't even say a word in the subway."

When asked if people riding the subway in New York, Boston, or San Francisco talked frequently, a number of students confirmed that Americans did not talk on the subway either. Indeed, those who had ridden an underground train in a large American city thought about it and confessed that they, "never thought about it before, but people probably never said a word to strangers."

The point here is that not talking to strangers in public places is quite common in most countries. But your new cultural lens forces you to see things differently, as if for the first time. Thus, it is easy to conclude that these experiences are culturally unique. Early observations will most often focus on what is culturally different, but it is important to try not to lose sight of the fact that all cultures also have many things in common.

Your new cultural focus will lead to many new questions about your own society. The discovery of a foreign culture will force confrontations with your own society's values, customs, and traditions. This is why many study abroad students report that they learned just as much about their native culture as they did about their new society.

This critical comparison between your new society's values and your own will inevitably lead to some appraisal of which society is better. This kind of reflection or discussion will force you to consider the dangers of both ethnocentrism and moral relativism.

There is no greater discovery during study abroad than to realize that there are different ways of living and thinking. The moral challenge of study abroad is that you are not afraid to weigh the pros and cons of each culture and then make your own personal decisions. Many visitors to a new culture fail to make such an honest assessment because they assume that their own ways of living and thinking are natural and thus represent the "right way" of doing things. This attitude defines an ethnocentric point of view.

A successful study abroad experience requires sensitivity to cultural differences. This means repressing your urge to shout out upon discovering a cultural difference: "that's weird!" It may be definitely different, but who is to say that it is "weird." Such a pejorative description suggests that your own ways are somehow natural and not weird. But you will soon discover that many of your own assumptions about culture are equally weird to the native population. In addition, you are likely to have to confront natives who themselves are guilty of ethnocentricity. For many American students who never really thought of themselves as patriotic, it can be a jolt to realize their own national pride when "foreigners" criticize their native country.

Being sensitive to cultural differences, however, does not require you to embrace every new cultural value or tradition personally. You certainly will, and should, make choices. You need not become a cultural relativist—arguing that all cultures are equally good. But experience in a new society should produce the realization that there are many definitions of what constitutes the "good society." Thus, we believe that each individual has a responsibility to respect his or her new culture and make an effort to act in accordance with prevailing customs and traditions. Discovering and benefiting from cultural differences is what makes study abroad such a wonderful intellectual, political, and moral voyage.

This adventure is more likely to be enjoyed when students can minimize the negative effects of culture shock. In this chapter, we have attempted to contribute toward that goal by theoretically explaining the reality of culture shock. Understanding why you feel the way you do is the first step to overcoming culture shock. Here are some concluding reminders to aid in the process. Try to maintain:

— the capacity to laugh at yourself;
— a sense of humility;
— an openness to new experiences.

You will make many cultural mistakes. Don't take yourself too seriously. Remember our earlier assertion that you are culturally naked in a new society. There will be many situations in which you will feel embarrassed over having said or done the "wrong" thing. Try hard to temper the consequent frustration by giving yourself permission to make mistakes and to laugh at them afterwards. We all like to think we know things about our environment. Realize now how little you actually know about most things.

Lastly, open yourself up to this new world. Understand that a new culture demands a readiness to witness and experience the differences.

The best way to begin this process of cultural learning is to write down on paper what you think you are witnessing and experiencing. In chapter three, we will explain how writing about your observations and experiences will lead to better understanding your new life in a foreign culture. But first, we must begin with the connection between writing and learning.

2

Writing as a Mode to Learning Culture

Why Write?

What does writing have to do with adjusting to a foreign culture? As you read this book, you are probably asking yourself this question. Isn't it enough that you have to worry about making new friends in a "strange land," exchanging money, perhaps learning a new language, and just plain adjusting to new people in a new place? Now, on top of all your worries you discover that you're expected to produce a lot of writing. Whatever for? Well, that's why we have written this book: to explain why writing about your new culture—from observations of street life, to various encounters with the native population, to what you learn in the classroom—is one of the best ways to understand it.

The aim of this book is to help you develop the ability to interpret your everyday cultural experiences. One of the great challenges you face as a foreigner studying a society that is not your own is to connect what you learn about the culture of this society, from books and other sources, with your own everyday experiences. As we explained in chapter one, you will discover that often your own experiences are a necessary but insufficient guide to understanding your new society. That's why your classroom is such an important resource toward establishing a richer and more complete portrait of your intercultural experience. You will learn a great deal about your new society in the classroom: its history, economy, art, government, popular culture, and language. But this knowledge becomes more valuable insofar as you can use it to interpret your daily life—from your social interactions with the natives to your appreciation for a culture that is rooted in traditions different from your own.

If culture can be defined as the unwritten and unspoken rules of everyday life, then we believe that the most effective way to go about demystifying these unwritten and unspoken codes is to write them down, give them a voice. As you attempt to understand the rules, traditions, customs, norms, and values of your new society, you will also begin to view yourself from a new and sometimes startling perspective. As we mentioned in our discussion of culture shock, some of your most fundamental beliefs may be challenged, at the least your assumptions about how to behave or what to say in a certain circumstance will suddenly feel strained, awkward, foreign. These are the elements of culture shock, but they also contain great potential for self-knowledge and cultural awareness and expansion. We, the authors of this book, believe that you are more likely to gain such insight when you allow yourself the opportunity to write about what you encounter. The very process of writing brings clarity to a thought; a writer doesn't always know what he or she thinks about a subject until the language begins to appear on paper. Thus, the act of writing is a process quite similar to the one you are undertaking in studying abroad: they are both acts of cultural discovery and self-consciousness—sometimes wonderfully exciting, sometimes painfully difficult.

Writing and Thinking

People all over the world seem to go through similar stages of cognitive development. As young children, they think on very concrete levels—in terms of actions and objects they have experienced. As they mature, they become more able to think in the abstract—in terms of possibilities as well as concrete reality. But some people develop these abstract thinking skills more than others. Writing actually helps us to develop these most sophisticated thinking skills. Writing is a means of leading ourselves to new discoveries; it is the act to explore places we never would have visited had we only thought about the subject in our heads. Thinking about things can only take you so far— eventually it turns into a circular action—while the activity of writing, on the other hand, advances your thinking forward by providing access to more complex and detailed arenas of thought. Toby Fulwiler believes that "When written out, thought becomes language with which you can interact; you can manipulate, extend, critique, or edit it. Above all, the discipline of actually writing guarantees that you will push your thought systematically in one direction or another" (19). Writing, as Fulwiler suggests here, is active thinking, a way of knowing: some theorists even believe that until we can express a concept through the act of writing, we do not fully understand it.

Writing and Learning

You've probably discovered the principle behind this point already, maybe through sports or a job, perhaps by watching young children at play. We learn best not as passive recipients of lectures and textbooks, but as active learners, making meaning for ourselves. Arnold Arons makes this very point when he argues that "As we look for improved effectiveness in college teaching and for the sources of our failures, experience makes it increasingly clear that purely verbal presentations—lecturing at large groups of students who passively expect to absorb ideas that actually demand intense deductive and inductive mental activity coupled with personal observation and experience— leaves virtually nothing permanent or significant in the student mind" (12). Writing is one of the best ways to create this level of permanence and significance, and to take control of your own education.

That's what this book is all about: the self-empowerment that comes from the acquisition of new knowledge. The more you write, the more opportunity you will have to understand better your foreign culture, your native culture, yourself. As Paulo Freire has expressed eloquently in arguing for educational reform that encourages greater levels of student dialogue and participation with the teacher: "In problem-solving education, [students] come to see the world not as a static reality, but as a reality in process, in transformation. . . . Problem-posing education bases itself on creativity and stimulates true reflection and action upon reality, thereby responding to the vocation of [students] as beings who are authentic only when engaged in inquiry and creative transformation" (70-1).

Writing and Organization

The human mind is a marvel unmatched by the most advanced computer. Still, most of us don't seem to command the kind of memory we'd like or need. Written language provides a "backup" for your memory and access to limitless information. When you have a lot to accomplish, you make a list of "things to do." When you prepare a speech or class presentation, you jot down main ideas, then reassemble them into some sort of meaningful pattern. Before an important telephone conversation, some people "script out" what they want to say beforehand. Combining invisible thoughts with the physical action of forming words on paper helps you discover, remember, and organize what you are thinking.

Writing and Perspective

Suppose you read an article comparing Italian health care with the American system. The author seems more or less concerned with establishing which system is better rather than with detailing the benefits and liabilities of both. By the time you finish the article your head is swimming; both cultures would seem to have their strengths and weaknesses. It's sometimes hard to figure out just what you really think. What can you do? Writing can help you discover how you feel about the issue. By listing the major points affiliated with each care system, you will establish a clearer grasp of the author's argument. Then, writing about this list will present the opportunity for you to arrive at new insights about the comparison. Most importantly, your writing helps you attain a certain distance—or perspective, if you will—from the author's point of view. While another author's writing may inform the issues you take up, the mere act of producing your own writing about them allows you to measure the persuasiveness of each argument, take a position, synthesize diverse opinions, disagree. Even if you fail to gain a deeper understanding, writing about the problem will reveal your confusion while posing new questions that may be worth pursuing.

Writing and Communication

Michel Foucault, the French philosopher and social scientist, observed that language functions to "tame the wild profusion of

existing things" (15). Writing brings order to the stream of con-
flicting information that our brain continually receives from our
senses. As you have just entered, or are preparing to enter, a
foreign culture, culture shock is an experience that is impossible
to anticipate. Culture shock occurs as a consequence of not
being able to order your thoughts and actions. Your frame of
reference is culturally specific; it doesn't always apply itself
well to a new society. You need to learn new ways of conceptu-
alizing and interpreting your experiences. It is through the vehicle of writing that we conceptualize, categorize, and organize
sensory perceptions into comprehensible patterns. Words are
the symbols of ideas and emotions. They are one way of measuring what we share with other people. Used correctly, they
convey thoughts, arouse emotions, motivate action. As Foucault
and others have pointed out, language may be the foundation of
culture, but writing is the medium that allows us to decipher its
meaning.

There are, however, different types of writing. The search for
meaning and interpretation actually involves utilizing many different rhetorical forms of expression. In fact, as you will see, our
conception of the writing process requires such a multifaceted
approach.

Types of Writing

Here is a list of observations our students made when asked to
address the question "what makes writing difficult?" Perhaps
you will recognize some of your own misgivings:

— The blank page sitting empty in front of me
— Knowing when to stop
— Getting started
— Knowing when to stop reading and taking notes and to
   start writing
— Figuring out what to keep and what to let go
— Remembering my purpose for writing
— Finding the time to write/revise
— Getting what's in my head down on paper
— Writing something that will sound right and not
   embarrass me

— Keeping focused on the subject
— Waiting until the last minute

All writers, regardless of their skills or accomplishments, sometimes feel as though writing is more work than pleasure. As one of our students remarked, "just trying to find the right language to say what you mean about a topic is difficult enough, much less producing several paragraphs that link ideas together in some sort of coherent form." We must begin with the premise that the act of writing can be, to a greater or lesser extent, difficult for all writers—including those who write professionally. If this premise is true, then student writers surely have all the more reason to feel constrained; most instructors require writing in each of their courses, and students are in the position where they have no choice but to write if they wish to pass the course.

The pressure that attends these successive academic rites of passage is probably not the best way to learn how to write or to improve one's writing skills. It is hard to get comfortable writing when you know you must do it—and often in a form that has not been your choice in the first place. The traditional classroom writing project, assigned at the beginning of a semester, often not mentioned again until its due date, and used primarily for <u>evaluative</u> purposes is certainly a partial explanation for many of the student anxieties assembled in the above list.

Clearly, writing is an effective way to reveal or demonstrate knowledge. But the main claim of the writing-across-the-curriculum movement, and one of the central points of this book, is that writing is also an effective means of acquiring knowledge. The critical question is what kind of writing best leads to this acquisition?

In 1977, James Britton established some helpful categories for writing according to the function it serves and its intended audience. He termed the use of language used primarily for communication—reports, proposals, memos, and term papers —*transactional writing*. These composing tasks were characterized by clear, credible, and conventional writing. Under the category *poetic writing*, Britton placed language used as art— fiction, poetry, drama—and found that these forms tended to feature varied and unconventional forms and styles reflective of the writer's imagination. The last of Britton's classifications, *expressive writing*, centered on what the writer wished to discover about herself and her personal relationship to the subject under discussion; it most often incorporated informal language that was relaxed and discursive. Unlike transactional writing, expressive writing is not concerned with standard grammar or punctuation, sounds like speech, is digressive, and writer-based—that is, the ideas and their manner of expression emerge directly from the interests of the author.

Several years later, building upon Britton's research, Arthur Applebee applied these same categories to the writing which students were asked to produce in American high schools. The scope of his findings, although confined to the high school experience exclusively, found overwhelming evidence that the most frequent use of writing that occurs in American high schools is transactional prose—and, more specifically, that 90% of the writing in social science and science fits this description. He could find no evidence of poetic writing anywhere outside of English classes, and less than 2% of the writing his research team discovered could be characterized as expressive prose.

Applebee's research on writing in American schools showed convincingly that the most frequent use of writing that occurs in the American educational system is transactional prose. Certainly, teachers assign this kind of writing because it is important for you to describe accurately events, scientific data, and various texts. Students need to learn how to write transactional prose well. And yet, while students have been required to write such essays, research reports, exams, and term papers in nearly all of their classes throughout their academic lives, writing skills have not improved very much in this country. Thus, teachers continue to voice their concern over the composing abilities of their students.

Educators have blamed poor writing skills on a variety of culprits: television, computers, telephones, and teachers who fail to address the mechanics of spelling and grammar in secondary schools. The list is as long as the lament. We would affix blame elsewhere: there is too much emphasis on transactional writing and not enough on other types of writing. The issue of improving writing and thinking skills is not only related to the frequency of student writing, but also to the *kind* of writing students are asked to produce. A sole focus on transactional writing is not only one-dimensional, but it also limits the potential for using writing as a mode of acquiring knowledge, and hence, as a discovery tool and means for self-expression.

We believe that transactional writing is a necessary component in the writing process, but by itself it does not promote critical thinking. If the student relationship to writing is defined exclusively in terms which relegate students to demonstrating knowledge of what others (scholars) have written, then each student's own language is only heard via a humble and passive voice. Now, please do not misunderstand our intentions here. Students do need to be humble in the face of what they have yet to learn from others—who often possess more knowledge— about a particular subject. Every mathematician needs, for example, to learn the fundamentals of algebra before tackling trigonometry. A music student must learn how to read notes before critiquing a score by Mozart. Our point is that students will be less likely to have a decent chance at becoming an influential composer, an accomplished mathematician, or a recognized scholar in any field, unless they become more autonomous and active in the learning/writing process.

One way of assuring a more active student role is to encourage young writers to engage their own language more imaginatively and analytically. Therefore, we believe that learners should often begin the discovery of any subject by utilizing expressive writing. Expressive writing is an important first step because it centers upon the interests and questions of the learner and thus leads to more active engagement with the material or subject of study. We recognize that expressive writing is often associated with certain disciplines—those in the fine arts and humanities—which focus more directly on subjective experience and interpretation. Consequently, many academics in the social and natural sciences dismiss expressive writing as inconsistent with their disciplines' emphases on objectivity and the objective world. We think this dichotomy reflects a false debate.

Recognizing the legitimacy of students' own interests and questions does not necessarily lead to accepting personal opinion and relativism as alternatives to careful research; in fact, we will show in chapters four and five how expressive writing can lead to better research. Beginning with what a writer finds most interesting or problematic with material under study is an effective way of connecting students to an established body of literature and research.

The opportunity to initiate learning by encouraging writers to ask their own questions and express their own thoughts leads to critical thinking and better writing. For example, there are many aspects worth studying about the American Civil War. One student might find the issue of industrialization as a key element to the conflict. Another student may be interested in how the absence of effective communication systems contributed to the occurrences of certain pivotal conflicts and their eventual outcomes. (The battle of Gettysburg, for instance, took place purely as the result of an accident: Southern forces were searching for a shoe warehouse when they literally ran into the army of the North.) Both of these perspectives might conceivably represent the interests of two different students studying the history of this war. In either case, each student would need to read about what scholars have written in order to deepen their knowledge of industrialization or how communication breakdowns often played an active role in this drama. Such reading should lead students to ask informed questions: Why wasn't the South able to compensate for its lack of industrial might? Or, in warfare before the advent of advanced communication systems, what was the role of luck or fate the further troops ventured beyond enemy lines? These explorations are more likely to be critically and creatively pursued because they reflect the involvement of the students themselves.

Students should not only master the forms associated with transactional and expressive writing, but also learn how to synthesize both. For the remainder of this book, we will refer to this merging of transactional and expressive modes as *analytical writing*. This form reflects a balance between the interests and active voice of the writer with an objective focus on the world.

Analytical writing is an intermediate step that begins to join the "I-centered" personal voice of a writer with the scholarly interpretative orientation of transactional writing. Analytical writing is centered on an individual endeavoring to interpret something; it addresses questions pertaining to the meaning and implication of events, observations, or claims to truth. In analytical writing, writers adopt the voice of a critical thinker, constructing arguments which are supportable by facts. Students who master this style, discover that writing can serve as a tool for acquiring knowledge, rather than only as a means for displaying knowledge. This is why we will be encouraging readers to keep what we call an analytical notebook during their experience abroad. How to compose such a notebook will be the subject of the next chapter.

The domination of any single writing style narrows the writer's potential for enjoying the act of writing itself; variation is just as critical for the writing process as it is for cooking. But given the type of one-dimensional writing that has been traditionally assigned in schools, is it any wonder that students tend to produce writing that frequently reflects a general apathy toward the spirit of critical inquiry and a flat impersonal style characteristic of a writer lacking commitment to the assignment? If the central goal of a liberal arts education is to help a thinker develop a wide perspective on the world, then educators need to look for more ways to stimulate this process. One way is to use various kinds of writing as a means for mirroring this complex world-view, as a self-reflective and open-ended cognitive tool.

Popular novelist Stephen King, in an interview several years ago, indicated that he begins writing fiction by placing a character in a particular situation and asking the question "what if?" In other words, King opens himself deliberately to a full range of fictional possibilities: "I'm like anybody else: 99 percent of what I do on any given day would not qualify for a novel. But sometimes the backgrounds of the novels lend themselves to my daily field of reference, and I draw on that stuff" (Magistrale 2). The point worth emphasizing here is how Mr. King uncovers that one percent of his daily experience has the potential to become part of his writing. How does he find this out? How does he recognize what to use? Partly, it is the skill of an experienced artist. But even the very best artist won't make these kinds of discoveries until he begins to allow ideas to flow by writing them down.

This is an important parallel for students discovering a foreign culture. You will ask yourself: "How can I write about this culture when I have no idea what this culture is about?" The way in which you begin to make sense out of this mystifying concept is to write down everything you think you don't understand, as well as what you do. You shouldn't be too concerned over sounding like an expert or scholar; in fact, as you begin the process of writing, you probably shouldn't worry about sounding coherent or consistent. But eventually you'll want to work at making sense out of these confusing moments—interpreting them by supplying some analytical context that lends them meaning and support. As a writer (as well as a traveler), you must be open to those confusing, but often insightful moments where "one's daily field of reference" can be translated into something meaningful. We promise that such moments will occur more often than one percent of the time.

Viewing the Writing Process

To illustrate the potential alliance among expressive, analytical, and transactional writing, let's consider the shape of the composing process as a whole. One writer may stress the value of revision more than another, while yet a third might argue for the importance of prewriting (discovery) activities at various points throughout the process. The point is, the best way to produce a final draft for any writing assignment might incorporate several of the following "categories" or stages of development; these, in turn, entail highly specific writing actions. While we are describing this activity as a "process," it should not be misconstrued as a linear process; that is, each of the following actions can, and probably should, reoccur throughout your writing:

Category	Actions
1. Starting	Lists, clusters, diagrams, doodles Talking with people Incubating on the run and in the tub (*Expressive "discovery" writing*)
2. Searching	Interviewing and asking Using the library Recording: observations and memory Speculating
3. Composing	Pencils or word processors Imagining an audience Connecting and focusing (*Analytical Writing*)
4. Revising	Re-reading and re-thinking Elaborating and supporting Getting Feedback Time away from a completed draft
5. Editing	Clarifying and combining Combining and condensing Rewriting to polish and perfect Proofreading (*Transactional Writing*)

As you consider this paradigm, notice the immediate positioning of expressive writing. Early use of writing in your analytical notebook is designed to get the process started; it is a means for discovering what you already know and still wish to find out about any given subject. And as we mentioned earlier, because this is not meant to be seen as a linear diagram, expressive writing might very well become a component part of each of the five listed categories. Such freewriting or discovery drafting is not only a means for commencing the writing process; it also helps in places where you are stuck or have lost focus. Expressive writing can even contribute at the conclusion of a writing project: writing to yourself about what you have actually written will often clarify your purposes. In fact, sometimes this "final" piece of writing will indicate that your work is not really finished, that you need to go back and perform further revision. But best of all, because you are already writing about these issues, the act of revising becomes that much easier; you have already begun the process.

Expressive writing is a worthwhile activity in itself. What you learn from writing to yourself will teach you something about the subject you are writing about, and in reading over what you have read, help to understand better the person who did the writing. This book demonstrates continually the importance of this kind of self-reflexive activity. But expressive writing could also become the first step in the process of producing analytical and transactional writing. Instead of waiting to begin writing until a few days before the due date of an assignment, or even trying to produce transactional writing spontaneously, there may be better ways of doing things.

Since formal, transactional writing is usually the most difficult type of language for a young writer to produce, it makes sense to start out less formally, with an emphasis on just getting the ideas out, issuing possibilities. This relaxed approach lessens the anxiety to produce "perfect," professional-sounding drafts, and even the difficulty that accompanies finding the correct word or phrase. This should all come later, after you have done some expressive writing to yourself in order to discover what you want to know. In addition, expressive writing is often a good way to break a writing block—just putting words down on paper, even if you end up only keeping a sentence or two, establishes a writing and thinking rhythm and instills the confidence necessary to advance a writing project forward. Whether you need to write a term paper, an oral presentation, or prepare for a written examination—virtually any kind of academic communication—the most effective means for composing is to work your way through the steps illustrated below:

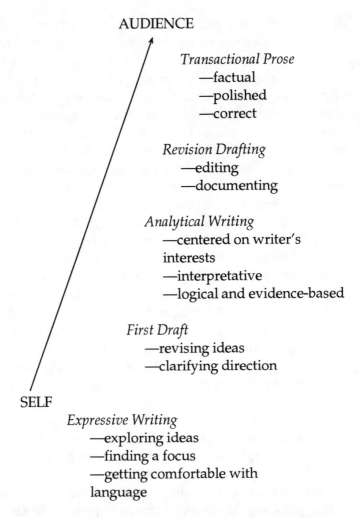

AUDIENCE

Transactional Prose
—factual
—polished
—correct

Revision Drafting
—editing
—documenting

Analytical Writing
—centered on writer's
interests
—interpretative
—logical and evidence-based

First Draft
—revising ideas
—clarifying direction

SELF

Expressive Writing
—exploring ideas
—finding a focus
—getting comfortable with
language

Many of the world's greatest artists, scientists, philosophers, teachers, and thinkers began their most important work in journals, analytical notebooks, and diaries. St. Augustine and Jean-Jacques Rousseau based their "confessions" on writing that first appeared in personal diaries and journals. Henry Thoreau's recorded observations on two years of studying nature and the culture of nineteenth-century New England led to his narrative *Walden*. Further, countless famous travelers—from Mark Twain to Anais Nin—have kept travel logs that became the source for writing that was eventually published.

Creative people use writing for the same reason we are recommending it to you as an aid to your studies: they wish to *freeze* the moment into language, to record their thoughts on paper so that they can push their thinking forward. The famous nineteenth-century Russian author, Fyodor Dostoevsky, produced elaborate notebook entries prior to and throughout the actual composing of his novels and stories. In the notebooks for *Crime and Punishment,* for example, the writer sketched ideas—some of them were worked into the narrative plot, others were discarded—concerning relationships between characters; individual character evolutions; the purpose and meaning of murder, both in the abstract and in the specific context of this novel; and the possibilities for directions in which the book might unfold.

As you read his notebook, it is sometimes impossible to tell when Dostoevsky was actually writing the novel (as whole sections of the published book were literally lifted directly from the pages of his notebook) or just speculating privately about events that would propel the plot further along. In the excerpt below we see both these processes occurring as the writer seems to wrestle with himself and his main protagonist simultaneously. The first sentences appear to be the random thoughts of the novel's protagonist. But notice how the writer continually shifts gears, interrupting both the actual narrative flow itself as well as his character's ruminations, by resorting to a kind of outline in shorthand. This is somewhat jarring for the reader, as we suddenly become aware that Dostoevsky is consistently merging his story-telling voice with another writing persona: that of journal writer speculating on possibilities for where to go next. Dostoevsky often used his notebooks this freely (frequently stopping to draw doodles—church facades, faces, and street scenes in the margins), to enter and exit the narrative text as he saw fit:

> The Neva. I wandered about. Insults. Why does that old woman live. Mathematics. I returned home. Scene with the landlady. They are going to complain (Nastasya said). Went out. Lizaveta.
>
> And it happened so completely by chance that I didn't think really that I myself would have to do the killing. Torments. Oasis water.
>
> The murder.

Panic terror, to Razumikhin's. Then getting well. Death of Marme-
ladov.... The whole perspective. Sonia insulted by Razumikhin. He
didn't answer the letter. Insulting of her on the street. At her place. Con-
fession. ~~Bullet in the head~~. Admit it.
Insolence.
> Sonia. Requiem.
> Goes to her.
> Scene with the widow Marmeladov.
> Quarrels at home.
> Fire.
> He brings a package to her. Say goodbye.
I can't live at home, unclean, disgusting, "If you knew!" She says to
him afterward: "We could not say we loved each other until you had
given yourself up." (55)

Novelists use journals and notebooks to push their work forward toward publication. But they are not the only ones who
think better through the act of writing. Great scientific minds
such as Leonardo da Vinci, Charles Darwin, and Ernest Rutherford left evidence of their earliest questions and speculations
that later became the basis for more formal theories and postu-
lations (see Strauss and Fulwiler 158-163).

Ernest Rutherford employed both a verbal and mathematical
lexicon to explain the mysteries of atoms—first to himself—and
only then to the outside world. He didn't simply arrive at this
knowledge; he needed help to get there. While he could assume
certain "givens" about atomic structures (the mathematics and
visual diagrams), he kept trying to advance his own comprehension beyond the known. This is perhaps best illustrated in
the written language itself—the two "Suppose(s)" that indicate
the status of his current thinking and likewise begin each new
venture into speculative territory (see graphic on page 39).

Similarly, Charles Darwin used his journal as a place to begin
wondering about how various acts of lime separation are
evinced in waters across the world. Did this separation occur
through the actions of water, or some other source? In his entry,
notice how he builds upon knowledge he already possesses to
ask further questions, which in turn will lead to new hypotheses
and an original context for comprehending additional information:

How is the Lime separated; is it washed from the solid rock by the
actions of Springs or more probably by some unknown Volcanic pro-

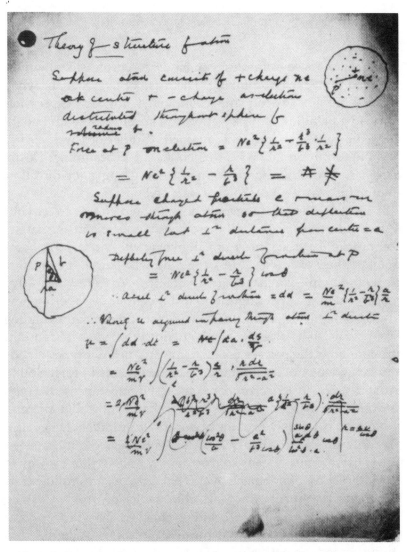

Rutherford's first rough note on the nuclear theory of atomic structure; written, probably, in the winter of 1910-11

cess? How does it come that all the Lime is not accumulated in the Tropical oceans detained Organic powers. We know the waters of the ocean all are mingled. . . . Have Limestones all been dissolved, if so sea would separate them from indissoluble rocks? Has chalk ever been dissolved? (8)

In each of these examples, you have seen professional writers engaged in discovery thinking. Their use of language, or whatever symbolic lexicon they employed for self-expression, showed a blending of observation and speculation with knowledge the writer had already attained. (Rutherford was clearly building on information he was confident in assuming; Dostoevsky, on the other hand, seemed to be groping for direction, finding his way with each new sentence.)

In the following chapters, we hope to help you discover your own connection to what all these artists and scientists share in common. Like you, these are thinkers who, at least at some point in their examples, are struggling with ideas: the creation of expression—language, mathematics, or drawings—that reflect what they are curious about, a means of discovering how to say something new, and an avenue for restating and building upon what they already know. Living abroad is a constant struggle with the new—new customs and behavior, new foods and language or at least idioms. Each day seems to force you to expand yourself to accompany social circumstances that you seldom anticipate, much less comprehend fully. But there is something extremely exciting about this cultural challenge; it is probably similar to what Darwin felt as he began to make sense out of those lime deposits or Dostoevsky as he wrote his way to the completion of another novel. The above examples illustrate the cognitive process; they are the results of minds pushing beyond what is safe, known, and established. This process is at the heart of a scholarly adventure. But it is also at the heart of study abroad. Scientific, artistic, and cultural discoveries presuppose that we accept the challenge that comes with trying something new.

3

Antidotes to Culture Shock:
The Analytical Notebook

Sunday morning in a sleepy city. I am standing alone at the Piazza Firenze tram stop. Around me the November air is filled with leaves, and the silence reminds me that it is definitely a Sunday. Suddenly, this orange tour bus comes out of nowhere and tumbles into a white Fiat sedan, spinning it like an empty milk carton. As if on an unseen director's cue, the sidewalk and street are filled with people; hands and fingers point at one another, everyone talks at once. Into this surreal dance of blame and counter-blame, I try in my best Italian to tell them the accident took place right in front of me: I saw it happen. No one is listening. My voice is another loose leaf blowing in the autumn wind. Inside an overheated tram car, behind a curtain of falling yellow, I rumble deeper into this strange city to which I remain so much a stranger, fully prepared to find it in ruins.

(from the notebook of an American student studying in Italy)

In this chapter we will apply the principle of writing as a mode of learning to the actual experience of studying while living in a foreign culture. Writing about your cultural experiences will help in the discovery and understanding of your new society at the same time as it enriches your knowledge of your own country and yourself.

Why Keep an Analytical Notebook?

There are many reasons, but the best have nothing to do with satisfying academic requirements or improving the quality of your writing (although these are certainly potential reasons). For a student living in a foreign culture, the analytical notebook is the best way of helping to discover, understand, and preserve your intercultural experience. Better than photographs or postcards, your own written impressions of people, events, food, and street life will serve as a more significant record of life in a new society.

Your analytical notebook also represents a means for helping to preserve sanity, to overcome culture shock. Anyone who has ever struggled to comprehend the workings of a "strange" culture, especially when that understanding necessitates communication in another language, can sympathize with the notebook entry that begins this chapter. In this entry, this student never expected his Sunday morning reverie to be so abruptly displaced. But his real shock appears to be cultural rather than visual: he expected people to be interested in his version of the story. In the United States, where he spoke the native tongue, people would have payed attention to his observations. But on this occasion, when he is so obviously a foreigner, his words went unheeded. It was almost as if he did not exist during the scene described in the entry above. The student's journal—or notebook, as we refer to it throughout this chapter—became a place for him to vent some of his frustrations and confusion and at the same time to reflect upon this chaotic incident in a strange city. The very act of writing all this down helped him to re-establish some element of control over what was initially an unnerving experience.

As we argued in the last chapter, when people write something they understand it better. In chapter one, we stressed the importance of *struggling* to understand a different culture. As such, writing about this struggle can be a tremendously useful tool in the intercultural experience, providing a place not only to record the diversity of this experience, but primarily as an opportunity to create moments of discovery, synthesis, and comprehension.

The challenge of intercultural education is to learn about the institutions and people of a different society as you gain a better understanding of your own country and yourself. Thus, the purpose of writing is both personal and political. However, the central theoretical challenge is to develop a perspective that allows you to understand how personal experiences are connected or related to the historical, political, and cultural traditions of a new society. The goal of your writing should, therefore, focus on *cultural interpretation*. This is why we are calling this writing activity an analytical notebook instead of a journal. The intellectual challenge is, in the end, to write analytically about culture.

Before you will be able to write analytically, you need to develop the knowledge necessary to explain theoretically *why* "things are the way they are" in your new culture. What you know or do not know about your new culture will obviously influence how you interpret your cultural experiences.

We have learned from studies in philosophy of science (Kuhn 1, passim) that what we *know* influences what we *see*. We do not see the world with a blank mind (*tabula rasa*). Our existing ideas, values, assumptions, and past experiences create a lens or paradigm through which we observe and interpret everyday life. Thus, it is not only our mind which is culturally biased, but also our vision; what we actually pay attention to is influenced by our own personal set of experiences and prejudices. Some students never grapple intellectually with culture shock because they do not physically *see* the ways in which their new society is different.

How, then, can we alter our vision and perspective so we are able to better discover and understand cultural differences? The answer is found in the classroom through *listening, reading, and writing*. The theoretical knowledge gained through lectures, reading, and writing obviously changes what we know. Not so obvious is that such a change also allows us to interpret more accurately our cultural experiences and sharpen our perceptions of culture. Insight into a new culture literally enables the study abroad student to see the world differently—to see things formerly overlooked or never seen before. Consider Sarah's comparison between the American and Swedish systems of public transportation:

> I've found that I look at certain things with an extremely American eye. For example, one of my first times on the subway I noticed that people could lie about where they were going (to pay less) and then ride as far as they wanted. When I mentioned this to my Swedish family, they said that they had never thought about it. I think that if we had this kind of system in the States, people would abuse it all the time.

The more you write (learn) about your new society—its language, history, politics, and culture—the better your position will be to understand it and become assimilated. This is why it is very philosophically naive to argue (as some students do) that academics (formal learning) act as an impediment to cultural immersion. Cultural immersion begins with taking your new culture and society as a serious subject of study. This means deciding now that you will commit yourself to using writing as a tool for better cultural understanding.

How to Begin Your Analytical Notebook

Your notebook is technically neither a diary nor a journal. A diary is a highly personal, usually very private record of impressions and observations. A journal, while still a personal document, tends to include references that go beyond the personal, such as responses to academic assignments and social interactions. The analytical notebook is more akin to the journal than the diary, stressing the importance of expressive writing as a tool for developing a more analytical understanding of your everyday cultural experiences. Whereas the traditional journal will sometimes digress into personal observations without a sufficiently critical context, the goal of your writing in an analytical notebook is always to enhance your interpretative capabilities. But as in a journal, at the center of this process are your own feelings, thoughts, observations, and experiences. As we suggested in the last chapter, the analytical notebook is the place to practice expressive writing—using language in a relaxed and informal manner—but always with the intention of eventually placing these personal experiences into a social and theoretical context. In some ways, the analytical notebook resembles ethnographic research as practiced by many anthropologists and sociologists, insofar as it records everyday life and seeks to interpret it.

If you feel like speculating right away about the reasons underlying your cultural experiences, do it! Do not be inhibited about writing about your impressions and reflections. They do not have to be correct. If everything we have said so far about culture shock is accurate, your analysis in the beginning is not likely to be right. The point is that beginning to write soon upon arrival in your new culture will help create a better understanding of that culture later in the semester.

Your notebook is a place for reflection. As a writer you have the opportunity to wonder about things, to consider the relationship among various aspects of social life for perhaps the first time. You shouldn't worry about grammar, spelling, punctuation, or formal usage that are so important when writing a formal paper or research report. The ideas that are raised in a notebook often appear as spontaneous thoughts, and placing the constraints of grammar or formal usage upon such a process can weaken the mind's ability to pursue digressions or gain new insights into the material. Therefore, write in a natural voice using your most comfortable language. You want to draw attention to your ideas in your notebook, not the means used to express them. Notebooks are places to shape ideas; worry about formal language later when writing formal essays or papers. Perhaps the most critical thing to keep in mind when using a notebook is that it is a tool, a means to an end, not an end in itself. Keeping a notebook allows students to explore ideas on paper without the risk of those explorations being marked up with red ink and returned marked wrong. Keeping a notebook is a way of learning, of talking to yourself, of exploring your own mind. Think of your notebook as a wellspring for ideas and inspiration; it is a place where thinking should begin.

The initial focus on your *own experience* reflects our pedagogical philosophy. As we suggested in the last chapter, we believe that students should be viewed as subjects and not as objects waiting to be filled with facts. Knowledge is the result of an active relationship between people and the objective world (Freire 75). Using writing as a means of creating knowledge allows you to recognize yourself and your social situation as central to the learning process. Knowledge about social life is never simply discovered. Rather, knowledge is a social construction which reflects the relationship between subjective experience, social structure, and history.

Thus, writing as a mode of learning is not simply a perspective or technique about writing. It is essentially a philosophical point of departure for investigating the world. Emphasizing the student's subjective experience through written texts is a partial validation of the individual's perspective on the world. However, living in a different society will demonstrate that a personal view of the world is not always a sufficient frame of reference for interpreting experience. The pedagogical challenge is to get students to test their own view of the world against those of others. Indeed, writing about a foreign culture will make a writer realize that many truths are not self-evident, natural, or universal, but rather, are shaped by years of exposure to the values and social conditions of your native society.

The experience of the individual, thus, is a necessary starting point but never a sufficient stopping point for social analysis. We may meet people as individuals, but to understand them fully we must understand how culture, history, and social structure shape their lives. Your notebook is the place to experiment with this kind of theorizing, by placing your personal experiences into a cultural and historical context.

What Goes into an Analytical Notebook?

The answer to this question is, simply, everything! We encourage you to write about your emotions, thoughts, and experiences. Use your notebook to *react* to lectures, readings, impressions of people and places, food, customs, cultural values, rituals, holidays, and even the weather. The fact that we are placing all this writing in an analytical notebook does not mean that the subject matter always has to be academic. The analytical focus, rather, means that you should always be striving to explain *why* you feel a certain way and *why* you had such an experience and *why* you agree or disagree with certain customs, rituals, or values. In the next chapter, when we examine one student's entire notebook, we will be able to demonstrate how this interpretive focus becomes the dominant theme of an analytical notebook.

As an international student, you are especially fortunate to be keeping a notebook, as literally your entire world—the everyday occurrences as well as typical classroom experiences and assignments—are potentially rich subjects for investigation. You are likely to find this kind of writing more creative and fun because entries will naturally reflect what is most interesting and relevant. Moreover, your studies are likely to come alive; what you read and learn about your new society may help make sense of everyday cultural experiences. Consider, for example, this entry written after two weeks in Stockholm by a student who has been studying the role of women in Sweden at the same time as she is herself a woman encountering vestiges of sexism in her interactions with Swedish men:

> In class we were talking about the actual differences we notice in society when it comes to gender equality. My first response was that personally I've never been treated as much as an object when I'm out. My main problems have been being touched by complete strangers—on the dance floor, for instance, where men just grab your arm and think you'll go along with them. At home, this never happens. All the literature we have read in this class says that Sweden is a country where women's rights are far advanced, but sometimes when I encounter Swedish men I wonder if they have been reading the same articles I have.

This student's entry is the type of writing that characterizes the effective use of an analytical notebook. Here her academic work is juxtaposed with the reality of life in a foreign culture. What she is experiencing on a dance floor with Swedish men seems to contradict what she is learning about gender equality in the classroom. But as we warned earlier, even though your observations may be correct, your initial interpretation may not be completely accurate. Let us listen to the same student two months later:

> I have been waiting to read this article assigned for class on "Sweden: Feminism without Feminists" since I saw it on the syllabus. I didn't think it made any sense. But after reading it and discussing it in class my eyes are a lot wider. The article has really helped me make sense out of much of my experiences here with men. Policy in Sweden is more advanced than the people. Women here are better off not because they have become feminists as women in the States. Women have benefited from the unions and the policies of the Social Democrats. Swedish women do have more rights; they are more equal in terms of pay, but there is, in some ways, more sexism because men have more sexist attitudes. That's it! I wasn't sure how to say it until now. I kept going back and forth about whether Swedish women are better off than women in the States. Clearly, they are, even though my own experience with men seemed to indicate otherwise.

Here we have an excellent example of how writing is a mode of learning. The student becomes clearer about the issue in question *during the process* of writing. This is a clear illustration of how the act of thinking through writing enables us literally to construct meaning. Moreover, this entry highlights how you need both the benefits of theory and cultural experience to understand social reality.

Even when you are writing about an experience or observation, and its meaning remains unclear, the fact that it is written down may help you better understand the same situation or observation later on. You may find yourself engaging in some cultural generalizations based upon one evening's interaction. The fact that you have recorded these impressions will allow you to compare them with similar experiences later. In doing so, you might need to adjust earlier interpretations—or perhaps you may even become more convinced of the truth contained and rendered in the first analysis.

An example of how perceptions change over time can be seen in this notebook entry from Steve, whose initial introduction to Sweden left him with a negative impression:

> It dawned on me just last night that I have not met many Swedes here in a casual context. It seems to me that meeting Swedes takes a lot of effort—and you almost have to have something in common with them in order to make that introduction. At a pub here during the first weekend in Stockholm, I turned to the girl next to me and tried to strike up a conversation. Wasn't trying to pick her up or anything like that, just being friendly. This girl looked at me as if I was crazy and said something like, "Do you mind? I do not even know you." After several months, however, I understood that this early interpretation was hasty, and reflected an American frame of reference: So, what am I driving at? It's not the Swedes that are so incredibly hard to meet—maybe it's the Americans that are slightly intimidated and insecure with silence. Sure, Swedish people are slightly reserved and a little shy in the presence of Americans. But if I were a Swede studying in New York City, wouldn't I think the same thing: that Americans are a little hard to meet when you are alone in a foreign country?

How to Get Started: Suggestions for Keeping A Notebook

We provide below a number of concrete suggestions for keeping a notebook. Your Program Director or professor may make some changes which best reflect his or her pedagogical goals and the challenges of your host society. But the following will give you a basic outline as to how to get started:

1) *Observations*. Your daily interactions will supply you with more than ample inspiration and material for writing. Particularly if you are living in a country where you are learning a new language, the experience of eating in a restaurant or riding public transportation holds the potential of an epic odyssey. Here are some examples from student notebooks that illustrate the challenge of everyday life:

> I just started to unpack my suitcases, and I was already depressed. So I thought that if I called my mom, that just hearing her voice would make me feel a little better. I went to pick up the phone, and I realized I couldn't even make a collect call to the States because I didn't know how to reach the operator. I tried looking in the phone book, but that just made me more angry because I couldn't read something that I had taken for granted at home.
>
> My first experience at grocery shopping was horrid. I left that place disgusted. I wanted to go home. I couldn't find anything I wanted. Which milk was the skim milk, where was the margarine, what kind of bread will I like, and what kind of cereal selection would taste like corn flakes or Musli? The cereal made me the most upset. I'm so used to a whole, very long aisle filled with different kinds of cereal.

If you fail to record moments like the ones described above, by not writing them down, you may lose the opportunity to remember them. More importantly, if you don't write about your observations and experiences, you may lose the opportunity for *understanding* them.

2) *Speculations*. Keeping a notebook helps a writer develop ideas on paper, helps overcome the fear of putting words down, establishes a "writing momentum," and allows writing to become a means for figuring things out—of knowing what and why a mind thinks a certain way. The analytical notebook should always be considered separate from all classroom notes; it is not just a record of a lecture or a reading assignment, but instead a record of what you, not the professor, are thinking, exploring, and coming to terms with in response to both your own cultural experiences and the material of the course. As such, the notebook is a place to take some chances, to risk without fear of failure or possibly displeasing the teacher. It is a place to make connections between the different topics you are studying and to connect your cultural experiences with what you are learning in the classroom. In essence, your notebook

gives you the opportunity to bring the diverse experience of intercultural education into a clear and condensed focus. Here is an example from Kathy who took information she heard in a lecture and applied it directly to observations she made about public behavior:

> I went to the university pub tonight. I noticed that Swedes sit down at a table and stay there all night long. They talk to the same people and don't mingle. Compared to U.S. bars, dance clubs, and parties, this is the complete opposite. I have been to a party here where there were only Swedes, and I've noticed a difference also. They also expect you to introduce yourself to them, not vice versa. I think this is a sign of their strong social network and personal ties.

3) *Responding to Class and to What you Read.* Just after a class concludes, when you have a few minutes between classes or at the end of the day, is an excellent time to write in your notebook. Review the material you learned today—reconsider the main points, their connections to what you have previously studied in this class and others, any problems you had comprehending the material, further thoughts about the topic, future applications.

Similarly, after every reading assignment, critique what you have read. By critique we mean simply re-construct the author's main points and then assess—critique—the argument in relation to your own point of view or the perspective of other authors you have read. We are not looking for mere summation here. Rather, the goal is to focus in on the central point of the article or chapter, and then respond to it critically with some type of interpretation or reaction and explanation.

Now we realize that this may all sound unnecessary or even "Micky Mouse" to you. The fact that as you read this you may be making a nasty face reveals how pedagogical traditions and school experiences have soured our attitudes about writing. Moreover, we are simply not used to using writing as a means of acquiring knowledge. You may start out feeling insecure about what you have learned from an article assigned in class, but as you continue to write about it, you may discover that you indeed learned a lot. The very act of writing can become a tool for you to develop a critical understanding of your reading material.

In writing about each class, you should also consider evaluating your instructor's lecture or consequent discussion. Such impromptu reviews are often instructive to both students and teachers. These after-lecture evaluations allow students to give a teacher feedback—to tell that person what has gone well and not so well—in a manner that gives the student an active voice in the classroom and in her own educational process.

Here is one student's commentary on a class discussion about the Swedish welfare state and the high taxes that are a consequence of this society's public policies:

> Today in class we talked about how Swedes are forced to pay incredibly high taxes which cover health care, education, care for the elderly, etc. Someone in class brought up a good point about the fact that Swedes must also pay to use public toilets, check their coats, or have a grocery bag. These things are considered conveniences in America, and no one would ever consider paying money for them. I am not a cheap skate, but why do I have to pay for such things in a country that prides itself in taking care of its population's basic needs. I don't get this. I wish we could have talked about this some more.

This is a good entry for a teacher to come across, especially if that teacher reads it before the end of a semester. For the entry is telling this professor that this issue needs clarification. The professor now has the opportunity to address it in class or respond to it in a clarifying note written directly to this student in his notebook. As professors of writing and sociology, we have learned a great deal about our teaching—what we do right as well as what we do wrong—from written conversations with our students.

4) *Cultural Experimentation.* In many ways your new cultural environment places you in a social laboratory. Your daily life allows you to discover and test observations and cultural generalizations. But it is a good idea to construct a few creative "research" exercises which focus on specific aspects of culture. For example, we think the following two exercises are helpful in gaining insight into your new society:

a) *Interviews.* Ask six natives (three men and three women) to identify and explain the three most important values in your host country. After conducting these interviews, compose a short biographical sketch highlighting the ways in which you think each person is typical or atypical of the culture and how he or she is different from yourself.

b) *Observational Studies.* Go to a main square, a cafe, a park, a concert, a sporting event, the theater or anywhere you can observe and take notes on how people interact. What appear to be the norms, rituals, or rules of the game? How fast is the pace of everyday life? How loud is the public chatter? Are people polite? Do strangers exchange glances? Do people obey street signs or other formal instructions? Look for answers to these questions and use your notebook to speculate as to the reasons for what you observe.

It is also very helpful to visit various institutions and organizations. Professors and study abroad administrators may help you arrange study visits in order for you and classmates to observe schools, workplaces, day care centers, and hospitals. Such visits are usually interesting and informative. But don't forget to write about what you heard and witnessed.

5) *Ethnocentric Moments.* Write about the times you responded to cultural differences in an ethnocentric manner. Writing about such moments will often help you understand why the cultural differences in question made you angry or upset. In addition, writing allows the opportunity to distance yourself as a writer from the emotion associated with the experience. Consequently, you will obtain a better understanding of your new culture and yourself. An illustration of this process follows:

> Things really take longer here as doing laundry, for example. Each wash is at least one hour and then I have to use a drying closet that I can't turn on because I don't know how. All of this would be fine if I hadn't been expecting everything to take the same amount of time that I'm used to in the States. It's difficult to always keep an open mind about things when something as simple (or so I thought) as doing laundry becomes a cultural experience.

6) *Breaking Norms, Customs, and Traditions.* This is the "stuff" of culture shock. Write about the times you find yourself unknowingly deviating from everyday expectations and people respond to you as if you were weird. For example, explain how others reacted when you put one hand on your lap at the dinner table, when you stood on the left side while going down the

escalator, when you failed to get in line while waiting for a bus, or when you spoke louder than others in a museum. These behaviors are typically American. Nobody likes to learn that his or her behavior is stereotypical, but use such social situations creatively: reflect and write about what such experiences are teaching you about yourself and your own country.

7) *Use your Notebook Creatively.* Experiment with writing for different audiences. For example, pretend you are writing a speech for an American magazine on foreign perceptions of American culture. Even practice some "analytical" letter-writing in your notebook: letters home to friends and family; letters to a teacher who would find your new experiences abroad particularly interesting; and letters to your campus newspaper, to your campus study abroad office, to policy makers in Congress connected in some way to your host country. Pretend you are the President of the U.S. and you are giving a speech to Congress on the strengths and weaknesses of American culture. Our point here is that as your audience changes you will take on a different voice in your writing. Changing voices can creatively stimulate both your imagination and your analytical insights.

Furthermore, employing variances in audience will help you see problems and issues from a variety of different perspectives, an activity that is fundamental to combating culture shock. From such an undertaking, you will gain a richer understanding of meanings and potential solutions. In the 1920s, Cubist artists deliberately fragmented and expanded the concept of "traditional" artistic perspective in order to create a multitude of perspectives. The resulting layers of angles and abrupt breaks from linear form were intended not merely to produce chaos and observer dislocation. Instead, the many perspectives viewed simultaneously on one canvas was an attempt to render a more comprehensive view of reality. That reality, in other words, could only be apprehended fully from a variety of angles and perspectives. Perhaps the same holds true in writing: the more a writer experiments with a wide variety of perspectives (i.e., audiences and the writing voices necessarily appropriate to communicating with each respective listener), the more likely his or her writing will approximate reality.

In addition, use *popular culture*—film, literature, music, sport, art, theater, television, and the mass media—as a potential source of material for your notebook. The dominant elements of every culture can be found in how human beings express themselves in the art forms stated above. Look to these sources for insights into your new culture and use them creatively in your notebook. For example, one of the most unique student notebooks we have received came from a student enrolled in an African-American literature course. After every two or three entries dealing with the material discussed in class or read as part of the course, the student would include a full-page advertising photograph clipped from some popular magazine. These advertisements always highlighted some aspect of race or interracial relationships in American society which underscored many of the social issues that were responsible for producing the poems, essays, and novels the class was studying. These photographs became a running commentary on the issue of race relations in the United States. Their inclusion became a valuable way for the writer to acknowledge the interdisciplinary quality of the material she was studying and, at the same time, an avenue for expressing her imagination and originality.

8) *Read Two Other Notebooks*. This exercise will help you develop a modest comparative perspective. It can be very helpful to learn if your friends are experiencing culture shock in similar ways or that your perceptions are shared by others. Conversely, it is important to discover if your perceptions and interpretations are idiosyncratic, and thus, possibly inaccurate. Each month share your notebook with two friends who are also writing. Write a review in your own notebook of the ways in which your own thoughts and feelings converge or diverge with what you discovered in the other notebooks.

9) *Critique your own Notebook*. Each month it is a good idea to read your own notebook and write about how your impressions and cultural understanding has or has not changed. This exercise will reveal very clearly how your cultural awareness is developing.

Well, I just finished rereading my journal. I seem to have learned a lot about Sweden, even in the past few weeks. I have the feeling that if I stayed here longer, there would still be lots to learn. Perhaps the greatest thing that's changed for me in my stay here is that I've learned to see things as Swedes see them, to understand their values and concerns. My first few entries seem to be about individual experiences—contact with Swedes on the subway, food, etc.—whereas my latest entries were more concerned with ideas and issues. I really feel that I'm much better at identifying with Swedes now. I do not feel that I am Swedish, but I no longer feel as though I'm in a foreign country, either.

As you re-read your notebook, we encourage you to keep the following questions in mind:

1) Over the semester, has your writing reflected a certain specialized area of interest?
2) Do you find a number of entries focusing on particular readings, references, or theoretical positions?
3) Where do you ask questions in the notebook—and have you already answered these questions sufficiently yourself or is there room for pursuing them in greater depth?
4) Which of the entries do you feel are your best? Your worst? Why?
5) Do these entries share anything in common with one another?
6) Where do you find evidence of critical thinking and insight that might be expanded into a larger writing project?

10) *When to Write*. Regularly! Not necessarily every day, but at least four or five times a week, sometimes more than once a day, and definitely after completing a reading assignment for class, seeing a relevant film, or participating in anything that appears to highlight your intercultural experience. Try writing at different times in the day—in the morning as well as at night. You do not have to write a lot each time, but try to write at least one page. The point is, the more often you write, the more writing becomes a habit—a familiar and less onerous activity—and a more versatile tool for analytical thinking and cultural awareness.

Writing and Language Acquisition

Perhaps there is no greater example of culture shock than the feeling you get when you hear the sound of words, but are unable to decipher their meaning. The communicative symbols of everyday life—words—appear as nothing more than noise when you do not understand the language. The reduction of language to noise is typical of how culture shock makes you feel like a child unable to comprehend "adult" conversation. Not being able to speak or to comprehend the language makes you feel alone, as though you were living in some sort of isolation bubble and had no business being in this place. For those students who must make a linguistic adjustment to their new country, the learning of a language will be the most important step they take toward cultural assimilation.

Writing in the language of your new culture is a powerful antidote to culture shock because it expands your ability to use the language as a tool for cultural inquiry and understanding. At first you will feel awkward both speaking and writing, as though you were a child learning to formulate simple sentences and remember basic vocabulary; you will be humbled and sometimes embarrassed during those moments when you butcher the rhythms and words that natives turn into melodious cadences. However, writing the language at least keeps your mistakes private, and more importantly, unlike speaking, you can go back and revise.

Moreover, the more opportunities you give yourself to practice this new language—speaking, reading, and writing it—the more proficient you will become using it. These different usage exercises are connected insofar as they all involve similar acts of language modeling and creation: teaching you how to formulate sentences, express yourself with a greater vocabulary and range of idioms, establish correct grammatical relationships, and conjugate the exotic verbs of your new linguistic lexicon.

Most people learn how to speak a second language before they are capable of writing in it; actually, this is the way traditional introductory language classrooms operate. Even so, we would like to reiterate what many language teachers now believe and practice: that writing in a second language reinforces and further expands verbal linguistic skills. Students who feel self-conscious about their initial language deficiencies discover that writing is one way to explore this new realm, to

become more comfortable using it, and, by immersing themselves in it, to uncover alternative modes to everday drill and
conversational practice.

As Professor Karen Sandler a teacher of French, reports:

> I have found that even at the most elementary levels journal writing,
> free composition, and other exercises that encourage students' uninhib-
> ited use of language to explore their thoughts can bring surprising
> progress in language learning . . . [M]otivated by the desire to say what
> they are thinking in their journals, students stretch their linguistical
> abilities to the limit. At first this means horrendous damage to the struc-
> tures of the language under study. But little by little, students come to
> depend on the language for expression of their ideas. (312-313)

Professor Sandler employs writing exercises at all levels of
language instruction. She asks students to make lists of new
words, phrases, and overheard conversation; to write spontaneously without stopping to correct or re-read for a fixed period
of time; and to create imaginative dialogues between people
pictured in French magazines and newspapers. Sandler's
approach to language development is to emphasize occasions
for play and self-expression. She believes that such creative
writing excercises present second-language students with the
opportunity to relax and get comfortable using words and language structures that are not only foreign but often intimidat-
ing.

Whether your current language instructor uses writing for
such purposes or not, we want to encourage you to practice
your new language by using it in your analytical notebook, in
personal journals, or in letters to other speakers of the language
you are studying. By writing words and phrases as you learn
them, you will be in a better position to master the language as
well as develop an understanding of how language is both a
reflection of the culture in which it is practiced as well as a tool
for deciphering the culture's unwritten rules of everyday life.

Many linguists believe that language influences thought
(Whorf 1, passim). This claim implies that language is not
merely the repository of thought. We do not place our ideas and
emotions into a neutral structure (language) in order to communicate with others. Rather, the structure of language actually

influences how we think. From this perspective, the more you develop language proficiency, the better your position will be to start thinking—not only speaking—like the people in your new country.

4

Interpreting Culture:
Sarah's Analytical Notebook

Much of what we have said so far in this book about writing and the intercultural experience has emphasized the important link between the daily experiences of life in a foreign culture and the act of writing as a means to understanding the implications of those experiences. The chapter you are about to read presents an actual notebook from a student, Sarah, who studied in Stockholm, Sweden. It is a document that exemplifies her cultural, intellectual, and personal journey in a new society. Reading the scope of her entire notebook presents an opportunity to witness how the process of writing promotes cultural understanding. In addition to Sarah's language, this chapter presents our voices as teachers and writers responding to her observations. After most of her entries, we often include two responses to her work: the first, which is presented in italics and set in the margin, is meant to create a personal dialogue with Sarah, to present the voice of a teacher responding directly to a student's writing in such a way that both affirms and challenges her. This dialogue is similar to what you might expect to find from your own teacher or program director when he or she asks you to share your notebook periodically. The questions and comments posed are not necessarily meant as criticism of what Sarah wrote or failed to write, so much as to provoke her into further thinking. As she reads the teacher's response to her work, future notebook entries should reflect the dialogical interaction you see beginning here.

The second voice, which immediately follows Sarah's entries, is meant to move beyond the student-teacher relationship in order to connect with central premises and points raised in earlier chapters. In other words, this voice speaks less to Sarah and more to you, the reader of this book. As such, you may find it less personal and more analytical in its response to Sarah's individual entries.

This chapter is about the link between reading and writing: Sarah is "reading" or interpreting the experience of living in a foreign culture; we are reading and responding to what Sarah observes; and you are reading what all of us are writing. This complex matrix underscores the intellectual challenge that accompanies the process of cultural discovery and understanding, as well as the writing process itself.

There are some other points to keep in mind while reading Sarah's notebook:

Her earliest entries are descriptive in nature. As her experience in Sweden widens and her knowledge deepens, however, notice how her language becomes less observational and more analytical. This process, corresponding to the pattern of assimilation, suggests the obvious: that the more you know about a place—its history, its customs, its language—the more likely you will be to establish a theoretical framework for understanding why certain events occur and, just as importantly, explain apparently contradictory experiences that differ from the stereotypes guidebooks and first impressions often foster.

Pay particular attention to the dialogue that is created between Sarah and her teachers. The use of an analytical notebook allows student and teacher to gain a level of communication—intellectual as well as personal—that is untapped in traditional academic writing. Her teachers have learned a lot about Sarah in this notebook—her writing reveals a great deal about her personality. The issues Sarah chooses to explore in language revolve around things that are important to her; however, her teachers need to keep reminding her of the necessity of measuring personal reactions against the rigors of social research. In merging the two, Sarah will emerge with a more accurate understanding of her new society and herself.

Sarah's evolution as a writer parallels the hope we all harbor when journeying to an exotic land: that early apprehensions will give way to cultural adjustment and political awareness, that personal confusion and awkwardness will eventually give birth to an enlarged sense of self, that intellectual speculation will translate into the confidence of scholarship.

September 2

In Sweden, a social democracy in which everyone is supposed to be fairly equal, contrasts stand out more than they do in the United States.

In the U.S., one becomes dulled to the homeless in the streets, one doesn't see the trash littering the ground in big cities.

Things I accept as normal seem out of place in Stockholm.

Odenplan seems to be a place of the abnormal—if after a week I am in a position to judge.

To catch the bus to Lappis, you have to go to Odenplan to get bus 40, which goes right up the hill to the supermarket. I have done this three times now. The first time I was too intent on not getting lost to notice what was going on around me.

The second time I noticed that Odenplan seems to be a homeless hang-out. On every bench, there were groups of homeless people.

The third time I was secure enough in my ability to catch a bus that I could really pay attention to what—and who—was around me.

Two homeless men and a homeless woman were having some sort of squabble. One man hit the woman, who then cried on the other man's shoulder. The first man seemed to apologize, and the woman leaned toward him.

For some reason, the first man got up and pulled down his pants.

The woman wasn't impressed, and got up to dance with the second homeless man.

They were all so drunk they could barely stand.

Early in this entry you say, "Things I accept as normal seem out of place in Stockholm." What does "normal" mean? It might be worthwhile trying to define what you mean by the concept. After all, would the definition of normalcy be the same for everyone even in the U.S.? This may begin to establish a point of reference for you to return to at later points in this notebook.

The first man got angry, broke the two dancers apart, then argued with the woman. He stood behind her, and pushed. She didn't even make an attempt at maintaining balance, and fell face-first in a fountain.

She stood, went to sit on the bench, and took off her shirt. There was nothing underneath.

Now I realize that nudity is more acceptable in Sweden than in the United States, but I am also under the impression that people do not commonly sit in public squares top-less.

This woman had no such impression.

The bus came, and I gratefully climbed on, relieved to have escaped from Odenplan (we now call it the twilight zone).

While these three people _were_ creating quite a spectacle, homeless people are something to ignore in the U.S. Usually they are so caught up in the crowds and bustle of life that they are easy to look past.

Not here.

These people were not standing alone on a corner, or sleeping drunkenly in an alley. They were right there, at a major bus stop, in a beautiful square, and they were creating a scene. In a warped way, they were making their presence known—believe me, no one was ignoring them.

The contrast between Odenplan and Kungstradgarden, for example, is astonishing. I suppose in the same way the contrast is huge between Manhattan and Harlem.

But somehow it's different here. These people weren't in a Swedish version of Harlem. They were out in the open, in a nice square with fountains and flowers.

The fact that they didn't "fit" made them stand out in my American eyes, made me see them and recognize them; kept me from sticking them in

In your discussion of three people creating a street scene, you write "believe me, no one was ignoring them." Can you detail this better? What was the crowd's reaction? Was it a uniform reaction, or did you notice some difference among individual observers? Take your thinking a bit further here. What do you think would have been the response to this trio if they had been on a corner of Harlem instead of Stockholm? Would people in Harlem be likely to pay more attention, or less attention to them?

the background as a sad, but normal, occurrence.

This opening entry is interesting because even after only two weeks in Stockholm, Sarah is already conscious of the fact that she is observing things with an "American eye." As we discussed in chapter two, the world is perceived through a paradigm, or frame of reference which is significantly shaped by one's own culture. In this case, Sarah realizes that in Swedish society the homeless "stand out" as a contradiction to the relative affluence of the neighborhood in which they were observed. In the States, Sarah writes: "one becomes dulled to the homeless in the streets," which makes the problem appear as a natural part of the landscape. Note also the way in which the notebook allows Sarah's teachers to pose questions to her that are intended to make her think some more about the issues she chooses to write about. In reading what her teachers suggest about revisiting her street experience, Sarah might begin to appreciate both the complexity of understanding life in another culture when viewed from a foreign perspective, and the need to "push" her observations toward a larger (theoretical) context.

September 3

The smallest things here bring out the ethnocentricity in me. I have few problems with social democracy, I don't even mind the sour yogurt Swedes like, but I find myself being critical of small and ridiculous things.

The escalators at the Galleria annoy me. Why have an escalator to one store? Why not simply have a second level of stores as we do in comparable malls in the U.S.? It's irritating and impractical to go constantly up and down to each store.

And who wants to go to the trouble of dealing with making a drink when it's so much easier to simply pour something out of a bottle? I

This entry shows some important things to notice. Don't ignore them—they are the stuff that makes the intercultural exchange something unique— sometimes a pain, sometimes delightfully intriguing—but always strange. In a

suppose it's all a matter of con-
venience.

In the U.S., we have two-story
malls with one (or two) main
elevators to reach everything, and
our drinks tend to come ready-to-
drink (except things like frozen
juices) with no extra preparations
necessary.

These observations seem flippant
and irrelevant even to me, but it's
always the little things that stand
out, that point out the larger
differences. I am completely at a
loss so far as to what these
differences are, why they exist. It
makes me feel like a tiny
child—noticing the things that
adults take for granted.

*way, you are a "tiny
child" in this foreign
world—discovering
things for the first time
and testing your
capacities for wonder.*

Here is an excellent example of culture shock. As discussed
in chapter two, the shock of living in a new culture reflects the
reality that everyday life is different. "The smallest things here
bring out the ethnocentricity in me." Sarah's frustration seems
"flippant" and "irrelevant" to her, but she is astute when she
notes that "the little things . . . point out the larger differences,"
even though at this point in her notebook she is unable to delin-
eate those differences.

We take the daily acts of life for granted because we accept
our own customs and daily routines as natural. When we can
no longer take for granted the stuff of everyday life, we feel as
Sarah explains: "like a tiny child."

The child analogy is a good one for illustrating the emotional
consequence of culture shock. When we do not know how to
manipulate the simple things of life—such as getting to the
second floor of a mall or how to make a condensed carton of
juice into something portable—we feel inadequate, like a tiny
child who needs somone's more knowledgeable guidance.

September 5
Swedish society is certainly
organized. Everywhere you go, there

is a number to take, a place to sit
and wait, and a flashing light to
show where you're supposed to go
when it's your turn. Everything is
accessible to the handicapped and to
parents with baby carriages. Street
lights beep so blind people know
when to cross the street.

Efficiency runs rampant?

I can't say that I <u>like</u> this way
of doing things—sometimes it seems
<u>too</u> orderly to me—but I do approve
of it. It is definitely fair; it
makes sense. I think it would
bother me, though, to be so precise
in everything. Sometimes all the
organization makes me feel that the
government is too involved.

The State liquor system makes me
uncomfortable. Alcohol has always
been something most people in the
U.S. consider a mere commodity, a
consumer good, available like any
other. Of course to get alcohol you
have to go to a liquor store (and be
21), but there are a lot of them,
they're not governmentally con-
trolled, they're <u>different</u> from
here.

It shouldn't make me feel this
way, I know, but sometimes I feel as
if I were in *1984*, and this govern-
mental big brother is there somewhere. I'm irrationally (and amus-
edly) afraid of the thought police.

It's interesting to approve of a
system on one level and to be wary
of it on another. I feel I need to
learn much more about it before I
make a definitive judgment, in any
case.

*Some things to keep in
mind as you continue
reading and writing in
this notebook:*
*—why do you think
the Swedes are so fond
of organization and
efficiency?*
*—what makes this
society so efficient?*
*—why do you think
the U.S. is, in contrast,
less organized or
efficient than Sweden?*

Sarah's observations are accurate and her comments reveal
both honesty and humility. Sweden is a very organized society.
The cultural belief in rational discourse and the political commitment to equality can be seen as underlying the tendency of
Swedes to organize seemingly every aspect of social life (Wolfe
132, Heclo and Madsen 3).

As we discuss in chapter three, humility is a great antidote for culture shock. It is important to recognize, as Sarah does at the end of this entry, that she still feels the need to learn more about Sweden before she "makes a definitive judgment."

September 8

Yesterday I had a long talk with a girl on my floor about the Swedish royal family. What would it be like to have all the responsibilities of being royal, without having any actual power?

Royalty, in and of itself, is an odd concept for me, but mere figurehead royalty is even more of an anomaly. (Is that even the right word?)

Hannah, the girl (woman, I guess) I was talking to, told me all about the things the members of the royal family have to do, all the remembering, do-gooding, etc., etc., to keep up a positive image. And for what? To be public relations figures, and nothing else.

Who would want to live one's life like that? I clearly don't share the Swedish perception of royalty, but I think in many ways they're (the royal family) a joke. It's a farce, all of it.

Maybe I just think of kings in a historical context, as people with rights and power, people who started and stopped wars, who sat on thrones and made decrees (okay, a little fairy tale, too), and this is certainly a pre-modern idea of royalty, but it's a pre-modern (an ancient) thing. If it's over, let it be over. If it's not, give the poor guy a little dignity, instead of relegating him to Miss America waves and a life of publicity with no trade-off.

```
    I guess there is a trade-off, but
I don't understand it. I think if
he's going to exist as a king, he
should have some power. If he's not
going to have power as a king, the
position shouldn't exist at all.
It's a silly exercise in re-living
and denying the past at the same
time.
    I have to remember to write about
what Catarina said about voting—not
now, though.
```

This entry is a good example of simply taking out your pen and writing in a playful manner about something that strikes you as "strange." You do not have to come to a serious conclusion with every entry in order to write down your reaction to some aspect of your new society. But for the sake of an argument, it would be interesting for Sarah to pursue the royalty issue a bit further. Do Swedes share her sense of cynicism? Do young Swedes feel differently from older people?

It is also interesting to point out that Sarah's last thought about the royalty makes her think about what Catarina said about voting. This transition is a good example of how the writing process brings ideas into focus. The idea is not completely explained here because we assume Sarah got tired, but Sarah does return to her thought in the next entry.

September 9

```
    What Catarina said about voting:
"I just realized," she said, "that
people in the States vote by what is
best for them."
    I nodded. How else, after all, was
there to vote?
    "And you don't?" I said.
    She looked surprised.
    "No."
    Catarina votes according to her
ethics, her morals, what she feels
is right, instead of what is best
for her.
    Are people in the U.S.—myself
included—so short-sighted that
```

Your discussion of Catarina and her motivation for making electoral choices is very interesting. Do you think it might have they see only their own lives, so self-centered that they are only interested in themselves?

Yes.

But there's more to it than that.

Our whole system is centered around the individual: when people vote, they vote for a <u>person</u>; the person they feel will do the best job for their own interests.

Here, people vote for a party, for issues they believe to be correct.

<u>Why</u> people see beyond themselves to the greater good, I don't know. At this point it is probably the national attitude that has emerged over decades (and may be declining, I guess) that persuades people to vote for other than self-interested motives.

But where did it come from? And where is it going and why?

Maybe immigration has something to do with it. Perhaps when the greater good applies to someone you don't think deserves it, you start to focus on yourself instead. But why would a person from Southeast Asia not deserve benefits, when a Swedish alcoholic criminal does?

So blood (and nationalism) that thick?

Probably.

Until Catarina said this about Americans, it never occurred to me that this is what we do. I mean, of course, I <u>knew</u> it. But not once had I considered it potentially incorrect. Flawed, certainly, but wrong? And what were the options?

It's amazing that people can live a certain way, think certain things, for two decades (and more), and never question them. Am I this idiotic and blind about other things? What a terrifying thought.

This, I suppose, is the benefit of travel and experience. And education.

What else am I missing?

something to do with why Sweden appears so organized and efficient as you observed in your 9/5 entry? It is important that you try to establish connections among individual entries. This will allow you the opportunity to understand how different aspects of Swedish society and culture are related.

You close your entry in speculating briefly that the reasons why Americans vote for a particular candidate may be "incorrect." It is important to point out that the goal of your intercultural experience is precisely to question (not necessarily to change) your way of thinking about such issues as politics. Studying abroad is always a study in comparisons and contrasts with what you know from home.

In the beginning of this entry we witness Sarah's discovery that self-interest is not the only factor that influences how Swedes vote. There is a clear recognition here how contrasting political values exist in the United States and Sweden.

We find, however, that it is her concluding comments which best illustrate both the nature of culture and culture shock. Sarah points to her confusion when she writes: "It's amazing that people can live a certain way, think certain things, . . . and never question them. Am I idiotic and blind about other things? What a terrifying thought."

Sarah is certainly not an idiot. The issue here is that we are all blind in a new culture and, to an extent, even in our own. We simply do not see or think about things we take for granted. As Sarah explains: "Until Catarina said this about Americans, it never occurred to me that this is what we do. I mean, of course, I knew it." This is a perfect illustration of how our own cultural knowledge is implicit or unstated. Sarah "knew it" on a certain level of understanding, but she never really thought it (voting solely on self-interest) was "wrong" or flawed until she learned that many people in other societies considered the general good before they cast their vote.

Sarah finds it "terrifying" to realize that she was "blind" to an important aspect of her own culture. This kind of discovery is at the heart of culture shock. As Sarah concludes her entry by asking: "What else am I missing?"

September 10
    The last thing I feel like writing about right now is a less than stunning article on social democracy, and I think this is a feeling I will indulge in at the moment.
    What do I see?
    —a small mass of little red berries
    —thousands of pine needles, all growing upwards, toward the sun
    —the mast of a sail boat and a yellow sign outlined in red that doesn't belong

—a rock the size of a dinosaur's
back—a <u>big</u> dinosaur
—inlets and outlets of Calon,
greenish-black water
—pine cones and moss
—microscopic purple and white
flowers that look like orchids
—leaves, blowing with the sudden
movement of soundless chimes
And I hear a rooster crowing somewhere far away. Where in the hell
<u>am</u> I?

September 13

A Review of Reading Assignment: Milner–Chapter 7

Milner spends a large part of
this chapter explaining the four
goals of the 1982 social services
act, and the ways in which they
have been achieved; also their
flaws.

"Economic, social security,
equalization of living conditions,
active participation in community
life, and self-determination and
respect for individual privacy"
have been the goal of such public
policy as pensions (ATP), child
care, maternal and paternal leave,
aid to the handicapped, and housing.

Milner then relates these
policies to an important criticism
of Swedish policy: freedom of
choice.

When I talked to the three Swedes
about their three most important
values—something I still need to
write about—they asked me what I
thought were the most important
American values. The first one I
thought of was freedom of choice,
of speech, etc.

Pension plans for the elderly are
certainly important. People of
whatever age should be able to
live comfortably, and after 65

*In your entry on
Milner you mention
quite a bit about
freedom of choice.
What do you mean by
this concept in each of
the contexts—Milner's
critique of Swedish
policy and the
American system—
you cite? I raise this
question because I
think it means dif-
ferent things for each
respective culture. This
issue might be worth*

years of paying taxes, they deserve something back.

Aid to the handicapped is also vital to promote an equal society with no prejudice and with opportunities for all. People with handicaps should be allowed to become active parts of a community and of a workplace. They should be able to live with as few inconveniences if possible, despite a wheelchair or other aides.

Housing is another issue Milner discusses. Housing should be available to all who need it, people deserve a certain standard of living, and if they are unable to provide it for themselves, they should get it some other way. Welfare policy provides that for people in Sweden. Income is not an impediment to having shelter.

All people should be secure in the knowledge that their children are receiving adequate care while they are at work. The other aspects of Sweden's policies toward children are good as well: paid parental leave, "allowance" for children—at least for their parents.

These are all things that should exist in a welfare society, I think. I approve of them, even admire them on a surface level.

Then the American in me comes out.

Shouldn't people have the right to decide where their child spends his/her days? Shouldn't people be allowed to go to school where they want to? Shouldn't people be free to choose where they want to live, and how?

I have that ingrained—and American—feeling that all people in a society are simply not going to be equal. I think they <u>should</u> be, but I can't imagine that they actually are.

exploring in greater detail—perhaps in another entry or maybe a comparative research project?

This is a wonderful entry, filled with the kinds of comparisons, tensions, confusions, and questions that show a mind actively engaged in its academic reading and personal observations. Maybe these issues will become clearer for you as you continue to deepen your understanding of Sweden; they may never be totally resolved, however, which is a testament to the quality of your insights and the difficulty of your questions.

Certainly everyone deserves the same opportunities, whether or not he or she is handicapped, whether or not he or she is from a wealthy background. And people are certainly equal on the fundamental levels of having the rights and basic needs.

But people are different, and though they may be all equal, what they want, need, hope for, dream of, will never be the same.

In America I think this is more true than in Sweden. America is truly an individualistic nation, and Sweden has a strong community attitude. But the members of the community are not all the same.

So there has to be some way, I think, of accepting the differences that exist in a society, of creating a community where there are options other than the one that is supposed to make everyone equal.

It does sound wonderful, this utopian ideal of equality, but Sweden is not Utopia, and that kind of equality doesn't exist anywhere in the world that I know of, even if it should exist everywhere.

September 13

I didn't get terribly far by asking three Swedes about the three most important Swedish values. Part of it, I think, was that they were all together and could make jokes and disagree.

One person quickly came out with "money," which surprised me, though I suppose it really shouldn't have. I think of money as such an American hang-up. I guess it's not.

With taxes as high as they are, money is becoming more of an issue for many Swedes, she said.

Another person said he thought that there were no important values in Sweden at all. He said that just about anything could be taken away from the Swedes, and if it were done by a shrewd politician, people might grumble, but they wouldn't really react.

The other two Swedes in the room were understandably rather offended, but they didn't immediately offer examples of things they would fight for.

Instead, they asked me about American values. And I realized that it was a hard question. My first thought was money, followed closely by the freedoms I wrote about earlier. After those two, it took a while before I feebly came up with personal success.

In the course of the conversation, the Swedes came up with the environment, education, security, family— all very <u>Swedish</u> values. Few Americans would consider the environment something to have a particular concern for, especially as compared to higher purchasing power.

Why do you think Swedes chose to emphasize the environment as an important value? Do you think Americans feel the same as Swedes on this issue?

My first reaction is to consider these values idealistic. But then I realized they are not mere values, they are reality in this country, things that people care about because they are a part of their lives that they want to maintain and protect.

Then I realized that the freedoms I, as an American, consider values I would not give up, are <u>more</u> idealistic; they are <u>not</u> realities much of the time. Certain freedoms do exist—like freedom of speech—but others simply do not. One of the things that struck me the most about being at home this summer was that I was afraid the whole time of being murdered in my car, or of having my house broken into. Of course these things were unlikely, but people have to be aware and cautious.

Regarding your final point about freedom in Sweden and fear in the U.S., is it possible to relate both of these observations to the issue of social equality you were wrestling with in your last entry?

```
    That is not so much the case here,
where the basic principles of
freedom—freedom to move from place
without fear—exist much more than
they do in the U.S.
```

This entry emphasizes how difficult it is to contrast cultural values. As Sarah implies, certain values may exist on an ideological level, that is, people may sincerely believe that everyone in America is free. And certainly many political freedoms in the U.S. are unequaled anywhere else in the world. But it is also true that the reality of crime and its consequent fear significantly constrains the freedom of Americans. This limitation on freedom, as Sarah's entry suggests, is perhaps not fully understood until an American lives in another culture where there are significantly fewer assaults on individuals.

September 16

```
    I went to a birthday dinner for
Catarina's niece last night. What
in the world is this birthday song?
"May you live to be one hundred,
then we'll shoot you and put you in
a wheelbarrow"?
    No one knows what you're supposed
to sing when someone turns 100.
    They had a big talk about the
elections, in Swedish so I'm not
entirely sure I understand, but I
gathered that most of them were
Greens—or at least leaning that
direction. None of them
particularly cared for the Social
Democrats, although Catarina—with
her characteristically low opinion
of Swedes—said that the Social
Democrats would win because Swedes
are too chicken to vote in anyone
new. I guess she was wrong, and her
family will be disappointed to see
the Greens out of Parliament.
    It was wonderful to have some real
food—though the meat was a shock to
my system after going without it
for so long. I keep telling my
```

friends that I'm becoming a vegetarian by default. Fish, fish, fish . . . <u>enough</u>, already? I'm going to go home a loaf of bread with gills.

Anyway, on the way back, Catarina said she thought things would have been different in the States if a foreigner had come to dinner. I guess she thought that Americans would all crowd the foreigner, asking questions, etc.

I don't think she's correct.

Her family was very nice, <u>I</u> thought. Her brother-in-law hauled out an atlas to see where I was from, told me about his travels, her niece told me about her year in Oklahoma—poor girl.

I don't know why everyone would drop their own interests to coddle me, when I was fine—better, really —just being a guest, a new person in the home. It did make me feel guilty that everyone had to accommodate for my language deficiency.

Somehow I get the feeling that Catarina is kind of the black sheep of the family. I don't think she sees the rest of her family very often, the result, probably, of her 11 years in the States, and of her awareness of her limited means.

It's interesting to be around someone who is so socially aware— and I don't mean politically cor- rect, I mean aware of social station and class.

Her family is old nobility, and I think she would prefer that social system still existed. She doesn't seem to like the fact that she isn't a member of today's upper echelon; she almost resents its.

It surprises me that she feels this way after her years in the States. Are people there that aware of social status? Is there really

that well-defined a line? Is there
here?
    If there is, isn't that against
the whole idea of the social
welfare system? How can there be
such an awareness of social class
in a country whose goal is equality
and classlessness?

Please note in this entry how a social experience—eating
dinner with Swedish friends—leads Sarah to ask important
political questions. This entry is an excellent example of how
writing about your own everyday cultural experience promotes
thinking about the larger structure of society. Sarah's ability to
formulate such good questions provides the opportunity for her
to raise them in class, to answer them herself in later notebook
entries, or perhaps to pursue them in other forms of writing
(e.g., research papers) or in personal conversations. In this way,
you can see how an analytical notebook promises to comple-
ment classroom participation as well as to supply the starting
point for more formal types of academic writing. (We will
explore this connection more explicitly in the following
chapter.)

September 18
    I really need to get used to being
in a big city.
    Kansas City is about the same size
as Stockholm—why does it seem like
a small town compared to this? In
Kansas City, I have never gone
anywhere (except on special occasions or for big events) and been
shoulder to shoulder with people.
    In Stockholm, whenever I go down-
town I feel as if I just stepped
into a mob scene. There are people
everywhere, pushing (albeit calmly)
to get where they want to go, waiting in line at the Bankomat
machine, buying things from a
street vendor . . . just moving,
moving, moving.
    Where do they all come from?

And why do they all look so young?

I'm beginning to notice that I don't really see older people around too much. And I don't mean <u>really</u> old people, I mean people in their 50s and 60s. Of course there are a few, but for the most part, there are young people everywhere, and only young people.

This makes me wonder about older Swedes.

I mean, younger people, maybe, have fewer commitments—both financial and otherwise—so they have the free time in afternoons and weekends to go out and spend money. They have the money to <u>spend</u>.

Do older Swedes not have the same monetary freedom? Do they not have the same amount of free time?

Clearly they have the responsibility of a family and a job, but many younger Swedes do as well. I keep thinking that maybe those responsibilities coupled with a higher tax bracket—I am assuming older Swedes make more than young Swedes just entering the job market—leaves them with fewer opportunities for leisure.

Clearly, I don't know if this is true. But if it <u>is</u> true, it's awfully sad.

Good series of questions here, Sarah. Particularly what you ask about older Swedes. But where would you find information about the financial situation of older Swedes? Also, do you think the behavior of the elderly in the States is different from what you observe in Sweden?

September 26

It really amazes me how much people here treasure nature. When they say they like a particular place, the first thing they say about it is: "and the <u>nature</u> is beautiful!"

I think part of the reason is that they begin to learn about nature at such an early age. They spend time in the woods, or on the ocean, with their families and friends; they learn to name all the islands, they learn to identify

wild flowers and mushrooms. Trees
are easily distinguished from one
another by age 10.

They also have that club to learn
how to survive in the woods—I can't
remember the name. But so many
people do it—it's a very transcen-
dental "one-with-nature" idea that
is a part of a Swede's entire life.

I find it truly incredible.

I mean, here I am, living in Sweden's biggest city, but there is a
beautiful walking path that
stretches for 10 miles—at least—in
each direction, going through the
woods, following the waters. If any
effort were made to destroy it
. . . actually, the most incredible
thing is that no one would make
such an effort. Nature is such a
sacred thing here. It is not to be
trifled with or destroyed—it is to
be respected.

September 29

Some of the happiest moments in
my life were spent on the Baltic
Sea, and now I am returning to the
water with the same salt content as
tears.

When I think of Sweden, I invari-
ably think of the Baltic, of crash-
ing against the waves on a windy
day in a wooden boat, laughing, and
licking my lips to find that they
taste like salt.

What memories this country—this
body of water—holds for me. Johan,
Magnus, Marianne, Berndt, Mats,
Asa, Asa W., Karin, PM, little
Anders, Haglo, Trompto, Lund, eating ice cream on the cathedral
steps, biking through the country-
side, tomatoes, Berndt Nilsson
singing drinking songs. . . .

Now there are three years between
me and the memories; three years to

idealize, forget, re-work the lines and actions—what were they really? What they truly were—whether I was as happy as I remember kissing Johan under the trees in the pouring rain—doesn't matter. How I remember them is the essence of the summer; what it meant to me, a character in the whole drama of love and joy and experience.

Three years later the waters are the same, constant in their teary saltiness, cresting at the same breaking point as before, and I am soon to be upon them again. But it is different this time. I am different. The idealism has merged into idealistic realism, tinged with cynicism, and not a little bitterness. Will the waters <u>seem</u> the same to me? Will they bring back some of the things in myself that I have loved? And lost? Or are they even really gone? Perhaps they are merely hibernating, merely protecting themselves from the harsh elements, waiting to emerge again <u>in the spring</u>?

Regarding your last two entries, I would simply say that if you live around beauty, and appreciate a daily concourse with it, I think your own per-sonality gradually bonds with it—a wedding of sorts, where nature is no longer separate from your life.

Sometimes your writing, as in the last two entries, can simply describe some aspect of your new society which you find wonderful, rather than problematic. The use of your notebook is not strictly limited to solving cultural problems or exploring complex issues, but also to provide simple acts of pleasure—recording, as we mention in the earlier chapter on using the notebook, memorable occasions that leave an impression.

October 11

I went to a travel agency today—a very interesting experience. Of course there was a convenient and efficient and fair "take-a-number-machine," so we took a number and waited our turn. There were very few people there (I guess not many people are into late-fall, early-

winter travel); so it didn't take
long.

When we got to the counter, we
realized we had made a mistake. I'm
still not sure exactly what we were
supposed to have done, but I think
we were already supposed to have
chosen a particular trip from a
booklet.

Culture shock alert?

Every time I have been to a
travel agency in the United States,
you simply say where you want to go
and when, and they make the
reservation, and it's no problem at
all. Here, however, it's not that
simple.

For example, we said we wanted to
go to Paris on November 2 (we even
gave a little room and added "or
3rd"). And we wanted to return
November 10 (again we were very
flexible, with "or 9th").

Not only were there no available
flights on those days, there were
no available flights to Paris that
whole week, perhaps even all of
November. Does Paris have a
"visiting Swedes" quota?

The same thing happened with
Rome, Milan, Madrid... we almost
went to Egypt, because the rest of
Europe seemed to have a huge
"STANGT" (closed) sign on it.

The next several agencies we went
to were the same way. We gave up on
Paris altogether, and settled down
to choose between the Canary
Islands ("When in Rome, do as the
Romans do")—and a tan—and Vienna—
and culture.

I think we're going to go for
culture; but we're certainly paying
for it. Not just for the flight,
but for the hotel and breakfasts,
too.

I could be wrong, but I think
that in the U.S. you have to
<u>request</u> a charter trip. Usually you
just book a flight, and that's

*This entry suggests
some of the perils that
await students living
abroad. It is a constant
reminder that the way
things are done at
home, seldom occur
elsewhere. But this
entry also imparts
perhaps the two most
important elements in
coping with culture
shock: humor and
tolerance. You exhibit
a good dose of both
here, and as long as
you keep summoning
them from a steady
reservoir, living abroad
will continue to
delight more than it
will frustrate.*

```
that. It seems to be the opposite
here. No one ever gave us the
option of just booking a flight.
    Perhaps this goes along with the
whole convenience and efficiency
theme. Instead of having to plan
all the details, you can just get a
simple package. But it also
requires that you're willing and
able to be flexible. Don't get your
hopes set too much on one thing
before you know what's available.
What you want might be "STÄNGT!"
(CLOSED)
```

Here we have a good example of how culture shock refers to the frustrations of everyday life. The simple task of going to the travel agent turns out to be yet another lesson in discovering cultural differences. In this case, as Sarah explains, many Swedes take charter flights when going on vacation (they are considerably less expensive). Consequently, many travel agencies offer only charter flights. It appears that Sarah has, unknowingly, walked into such an agency.

If this whole story seemed irrelevant to you as you read her entry, we bet that you have not been living in your new society for very long. On the other hand, if you have been living abroad for some time, you were probably laughing in empathy with Sarah's particular situation.

October 12

```
    I had forgotten, until recently,
about name days. The last time I
was at my contact mother's I was
getting something out of the
refrigerator, and found myself face
to face with a calendar. On every
day were three or four names.
    In an instant, I was flooded with
memories. The summer I spent living
with a family in Southern Sweden,
my name day was July 19. I had been
with the family for two weeks. We
got along wonderfully.
```

When I woke up that morning and walked into the living room, the first thing they said was "Happy name day."

I had <u>no</u> idea what they were talking about. What in the world is a <u>name</u> <u>day</u>? My host brother, Magnus, explained it to me, but I still thought he was joking, until my host father reaffirmed his explanation.

Then I saw that Marianne (my host mom) had a pile of wild flowers in front of her, and was in the process of making a garland. When it was done, she put it on my head. The neighbors came over, and we all had waffles with strawberry jam.

It wasn't a <u>huge</u> deal that it was someone's name day, but it was a perfect excuse to be merry, to see your friends, and have a good time. Name days, I think, are one of the loveliest traditions in Sweden. There are too few things to celebrate on a day-to-day basis as it is—name days bring a few days of happiness to every year that wouldn't be there without them.

As for how this reflects on Swedish society, the tradition—if I remember correctly—emerged when days were given the names of saints. What was done initially to honor the saints, then extended to become a holiday for people whose names were those of the saints. People began to name their children according to what day they were born on. New names have been incorporated into the calendar ever since.

I guess this shows the Swedish tie to Lutheranism—a celebration of saints. The Lutheran ethos seems to exist in so many facets of Swedish life—it's something we focus on in my literature class. Lutheranism and nature—sometimes I think this

whole society is rooted in one or
the other.

This is another illustration of how learning about your host
country in the classroom—in this case it is the influence of the
Lutheran ethos—can be helpful in interpreting cultural
customs.

October 18

I never want to eat chocolate
again.

The trip to Marabou (a chocolate
company) was yesterday, and I still
haven't recovered. From the moment
we got there (once we had donned
our lovely white net Marabou hats
and jackets) we were eating chocolate—light chocolate, dark chocolate, Daions chocolate with nuts,
chocolate with caramel, chocolate
with fruit. . . . What I'm getting
at is that we ate rather a lot of
chocolate.

But Marabou was everything a
Swedish company should be. I've
never been in a factory before, so
I don't really have anything to
concretely compare it to, but I
think I would much rather work at
Marabou than at an American factory
(which I imagine to be rather
dirty, dark, and generally
unhealthy). At Marabou there was
light everywhere—even on a rainy
day. On a sunny day, it would have
been beautiful—at least the view.
The factory was clean—how is it
possible to keep a factory <u>clean</u>?

One thing I found particularly
interesting was that employees
rotate every half hour (if I
remember the time correctly). This
strikes me as particularly Swedish.
In the U.S., an employer would
argue that by being at the same
machine all the time a given worker

*In the literature you
have been reading so
far this semester, what
have the authors writ-
ten about industrial
and labor relations in
Sweden that might be
added to your present
observations about
Marabou so as to root
them in a theoretical
framework? More sim-
ply stated, why is the
"whole principle dif-
ferent here"? What
is the relationship
between working condi-
tions and productivity?*

is best at that given job and
should therefore stay there.
Whether or not his employees are
bored to death automatons is irrelevant to the employer as long as
production is high. The whole principle is different here. Employees
are not just part of the machine,
they are actually treated as human
beings. And as human beings they
have the right to be as comfortable
in their jobs as possible.

*I think this entry is
filled with possibilities
for further writing. A
place to start is with
the questions asked
above.*

So employers take the extra time
to teach people how to use more
than one machine, they take the
time to improve the job setting and
the job itself. It's really very
impressive.

I think companies in the U.S.
would profit by paying attention to
this particular aspect of the
Swedish model.

October 19

I went to Pizza Hut today. It was
painful. It's the first real pizza
I've had since I got here—not that
sauce and vegetables on cardboard
stuff—and it was almost perfect. It
wasn't quite like the pizza at
home, but it was close.

As I sat there, eating real pizza
(why do I always feel the urge to
capitalize that word?) and listening to real American music, I
really felt that I could have been
at home. I could ignore the fact
that all the women had mismatched
scrunchies in their hair, with
tendrils poking out in the most
interesting places. I could ignore
that children were allowed to crawl
wildly about with next to no super-
vision. I could ignore that everyone was in Levis. I could even
close my ears to the foreign
language being spoken around me.

It was a wonderful—if deluded—
feeling.

Then I went to the bathroom. No
matter what else I may be able to
ignore, I simply cannot ignore
those damn toilets. All my delu-
sions faded away, and I knew once
again that I was in Sweden.

This is not to say that I could
no longer enjoy the pizza or the
atmosphere. Just not with the same
wholly American feel. The
scrunchies began to annoy me, the
children—I thought—really should
be done something with, and the
Levis . . . what can you do? And I
realized, once again, that 9/10 of
the conversation around me was off-
limits because of my language
restrictions.

It was like culture shock,
reverse culture shock, and culture
shock all crammed into the space of
an hour.

But the pizza was still good!

One day after observing a factory "like a Swede" (October 18 entry), Sarah finds herself feeling the effects of culture shock. As we have explored in chapter three, typical of culture shock is both a yearning for the familiar—"pizza and real American music"—and anger at what is perceived to be foreign. Cultural adjustment and integration is always an uneven—two steps back for every one step forward—dance.

October 21

The first question we were asked
at the gymnasium (a Swedish high
school) today was: "How many television stations do you have?"

I was sitting there expecting
something political, or something
about the American education system, and instead we got TV! The
Swedes were amazed at the extent of
good old American cablevision,
which can provide upwards of 70

stations. Why, they asked, would anyone <u>want</u> so many television stations?

As an American, my response (though I didn't say this) was "Why not? If you <u>can</u> have them, why not?" It struck me as typically American that my gut reaction was based on the hours of enjoyment to be attained from cablevision and the educational opportunities available in many of its stations (both questionable anyway) but instead on the idea of simply having something because you <u>can</u> have it. It was a very materialistic response that I've been flogging myself for ever since. Part of it is due to the fact that neither of my parents has ever gotten cable, something that frustrated and annoyed me for most of my teenage years. But part of it is indeed materialism, keeping up with the Joneses.

The other hysterical question we got was aimed at Ingrid, who had mentioned that she is from Ohio. One skinny (of course) Swedish girl raised her hand and said "You're from Ohio?" Ingrid nodded. The girl went on, "Do you know Susan Anderson?" Excuse me?

Needless to say, Ingrid didn't.

But the question itself showed an interesting perception of the United States. Everyone knows what a big country it is, but maybe they don't have the same perception of individual states being rather large as well. Of course part of the impetus behind the question was probably the same thinking that makes me ask someone who goes to a big state school if they know someone I know who goes there, when the chances of that happening are about 1 in 20,000. People like to feel that they have something in common with other people, that there is a

This is an example of a self-reflective moment that can only occur when you are living abroad. The issue—and your related discussion of it—simply would be less likely to take place with your American friends. Many would probably just assume that seventy cable stations was another step in technological advancement.

tie somewhere, and that the world
isn't so large as it can seem. But
that girl's question threw us all
momentarily off balance.

I am really glad we got the
opportunity to go to a gymnasium—
even though I didn't get a musical
class—and see Swedish students at
work. We did get serious questions
about politics and AIDS education,
etc. I think I learned a lot about
Swedish teenagers' perception of
the States—unfortunately most of
them were rather off-kilter. They
seemed to think everyone in the
States was high on drugs about 90-
95% of the time, and that all
everyone does is sit around and eat
McDonald's and watch TV. They're a
little too close to being right for
my comfort, but they weren't as
right as they seemed to think they
were. We do, after all, have to
walk from our houses to our cars,
if no farther.

This entry was written after a visit to a Swedish high school.
It is interesting to note here that, even though we have advised
you to avoid easy generalizations about cultural life in your
new society, many natives are obviously not so well instructed.
Consequently, you may meet many people who will make
statements about your own country which are overstated or
untrue. The Swedish high school students Sarah encountered
are clear examples of this tendency.

October 23

How do Swedes dress so well? So
much of their income goes to taxes,
food is incredibly expensive,
everything else is incredibly
expensive, where do they find the
money to spend $100 on Levis? (Why
is another question).

With very few exceptions, Swedes
dress very well. But every time I

go to the department store I blanch
when I see price tags. Just today I
saw a bodysuit that I would have
priced at maybe 200 kronor marked
at over three times that. Who could
possibly afford that? But Swedes
seem to manage.

I suppose part of it may be that
Swedes do have fewer clothes than
Americans. Swedes seem to be amazed
at the amount of clothes Americans
have. And of course they don't mind
wearing the same thing for days in
a row. So I guess they don't need
as much. But they also seem to keep
up so closely on all the newest
fashions.

It amazes me, too, that people
who so clearly care about their
appearance from the neck down (I am
speaking specifically about women,
here) can throw their hair up in a
randomly placed assortment of
clashing scrunchies and/or
barrettes with whole clumps of hair
falling out of place, and go <u>out</u>
like that. From the neck down they
look as if they were ready to
impress even the most critical
observer. But from the neck up they
look like a hairdresser's worst
nightmare. Why?

It's as if they didn't want to
look <u>too</u> perfect. I guess the rest
of us should appreciate it.

*Interesting. But my
impression is that
many Swedish women
do "care" about their
hair. Is it possible that
the "style" you have
critiqued is in fact an
intentional "look"?*

One of the more interesting aspects of using an analytical
notebook is when reader (the professor or another student) and
writer disagree. The resulting dialogue is not only fun to read, it
also serves as a reminder of the difficulty of interpreting observations in a new culture: we don't always agree about what we
see or how we interpret these observations.

October 31
We saw a Bergman production of
Peer Gynt last night. It was abso-

lutely incredible. But what will stick in my memory most is not the directing, not the acting, but in one rather unusual prop: an over-sized, plastic (I hope) erect penis.

Shocking isn't it? As an American, you're supposed to be stunned that such a thing was on a stage where, over the course of this play's run, thousands of people will see it.

It was incredibly funny, and it underlined for me one of the big cultural differences between Sweden and America: views towards sexuality.

The Swedes in the audience were shocked, too, but mainly they found it to be amusing. The shock wasn't a disapproving shock, but just a surprise because it was unexpected.

Me, however—the whole time, all I could think was "This would never float on an American stage." I was in a play last semester about homosexuality and sexual freedom and some old women walked out on what they considered to be a particularly dirty line, and that was just words—not an actual physical exhibit. Actual nakedness—even plastic nakedness—would have put them in the hospital.

The reason for this difference, I believe, is a completely different attitude about sex and the human body. Americans view sex as something to either be joked about or discussed behind closed—and locked—doors, and the body as something to hide in all situations (except *Obsession* ads).

Swedes, on the other hand, accept sex as a fact of life—as necessary to life—and the body is not as shameful as it is in the U.S. Maybe this is because all Swedes have such good bodies, but whatever the reason, they are much less tense

This discussion regarding differing cultural perceptions of sexuality is a complex one. You might consider pursuing it further—perhaps in a more formal essay? The reason for the difference you observe in this entry may have to do with varying religious backgrounds (i.e., Puritanism was never the force in Sweden that it was, and still to some residue extent is, in the United States); the association between violence and sexuality that is a problem in the States but, less so in Sweden; and various other issues that would be worth your time exploring.

about the whole concept of sexuality.
   This kind of freedom, it seems,
leads to freedom in other areas of
life. It allowed Bergman to express
this certain act as fully and
pointedly (no pun intended) as he
wanted to.
   P.S. Happy Halloween!

The point to emphasize here is that in viewing a play which
Sarah found "absolutely incredible," what stuck in her memory
the most was what she perceived to be a cultural difference in
attitudes toward sexuality. If we were to examine another
student's analytical notebook, we might discover that that
person's response to this play had nothing to do with sexuality
and culture, but instead focused on something else. Neither
focus is "wrong"—the notebook merely allows you the opportunity to pursue what you find most interesting.

November 1
   Well, I celebrated my first major
holiday away from home yesterday—a
Halloween in the land of trolls. It
was very strange. It didn't really
feel like it was Halloween; there
were no ghosts hung in windows, no
witches, no jack-o-lanterns.
   All I can say is thankfully there
was the Halloween party to look
forward to. It was something to
prepare for, something to build
anticipation for.
   Holidays—both Swedish and American—are when I feel most removed
from this society. On Halloween I
felt so far away from my family and
friends, from traditions that I
grew up with. On Swedish holidays I
feel like such an outsider. It's
less a matter of not celebrating
the same things than simply not
knowing what is being celebrated.
Why are things closed early on a
given day? Why do people dress
differently on another day?

The party was different, though.
All of a sudden Swedes and Americans alike were on the same wave-
length. Maybe—probably—it was the
ample supply of beer, but it was
comforting. Swedes were in
costumes, Americans were in costumes . . . everyone wanted to
celebrate. Once we were on that
equal ground, it really didn't matter that I wasn't at home; it
really didn't matter that Swedes
don't celebrate Halloween.

A common culture is what creates solidarity and community
among individuals. Holidays are the best symbols of a culture's
celebration or ritual of a shared political or religious belief, fear,
or simple custom or tradition. Therefore, it makes sense that
holidays would make Sarah feel especially alienated. As was
the case with this particular incident, organizing a party for the
natives to celebrate one of your own holidays can be a creative
way of turning a depressing day into a memorable one in which
you share your culture with others.

November 7 (On Vacation in Vienna)
I bought this pen at the Sigmund
Freud museum today. I have a feeling it will be one of those pens I
really enjoy writing with. I don't
want to write a real entry now—just
wanted to get some words on paper.
Right now it's nap time! I could
get used to this.
Time for a real entry.
We were going to sleep late this
morning, after our night on the
town last night, but ended up
getting out of bed at 8:20 and down
to breakfast by 9:20 or so. I'm so
impressed by our <u>drive</u> this week.
We haven't slept in once, we've
spent every day at worthwhile
places, on worthwhile pursuits.
It's that we know we only have a
short time, and we want to experi-

ence <u>everything</u>. So far we're doing a great job.

After breakfast we took the train to the ring, walked around the park with the Mozart monument, saw the Goethe monument, Parliament, the university, the Rathaus, Freud Park, Votir church and the Freud museum.

In the part with the Mozart monument, we saw an older woman walking quite rigidly, dressed to a tee, and looking as if she were too good to smile. She looked like millions of upper-class middle-aged women around the globe. <u>Except</u> she was playing "fetch" with her perky little black dog. It was a very unique night—rather dichotomous— but wonderful. When her dog would come bounding back with the ball, she would smile ever so slightly, reach down to her dog, and throw the ball again, walking on the whole time.

Anyway—we couldn't go into the Parliament building, though it was impressive enough from the outside. The university was incredible—we did go in there, and I almost wished we hadn't. It was <u>majestic</u>. Then I went into the bathroom and realized that everything has a bad side (what a pit!). Stockholm University may not be the most majestic place on earth, but the country it's in, the city it's in, are great. If I weren't there, I would never have known the people I know now, people I hope to know for the rest of my life.

Last night we all had a toast before we went out. Mine was: "To friends you make in Sweden and keep forever." Cheezy, I know.

None of us knew what the Rathaus was, so we didn't go in there. It's probably the most important build- ing in Vienna or something, but someday I'll come back again.

Then we went to the Sigmund Freud
park. On the way we went to Grillparzer Street so I could take a
picture of the street sign. There
was no Pension Grillparzer. Sorry,
Garp.

The Freud museum was really
interesting. I bought this pen
there. Red. I think Freud would
approve. On the way out we met a
guy from South Africa, because he
asked Amber to take a picture of
him in front of the museum. We saw
him again in the subway station and
started talking to him. <u>That</u> was
actually when we found that he was
from South Africa. We talked for a
while, then he asked if we wanted
to get together tonight. He's traveling alone, and hasn't spoken to
anyone in three weeks. There are
three of us—what could he do? So
we made plans to meet outside
Stephansdom.

Then we ate lunch (at the McDonald's, of course) came home, wrote
postcards, took a nap, then met
Gary (Pfiffer, his name) at 7:30.
We went to a club called Jazzland,
where we ate Austrian food (dump-
lings with eggs—or the other way
around, really) and talked. Then we
had to pay 100 shillings to stay
for the band, which we couldn't
afford, so we went to a place
called the Tunnel. It seemed to be
quite the hot spot. I never thought
smoke could really irritate my
eyes, but <u>wow</u>—<u>ouch</u>. We left at
about 10:30, now it's 11:30, and
we're home safe and sound.

It was really interesting to talk
to Gary. He told us a lot about the
political situation in South
Africa, and said he was optimistic
about the future, which was very
comforting to hear. He said the
economic sanctions really spurred
the changes there, as well as
deKlerk's leading the government.

Of course, as a white South African it is probably easy for him to be positive. But he has close ties to the ANC, seemed very educated, and could back his opinion up very well. I hope he's right.

On the way home, we talked about what a great experience this trip has been. We have broadened our horizons so much, learned so much; I feel that today I really experienced the benefits of traveling. We met someone new from an entirely different world, we got to know him (a little, at least), and saw that everyone is really the same; at the same time we learned about the differences and similarities of our respective cultures.

My perceptions of a whole country have changed today. Everything I knew before was based on one-sided media. Today I learned something first-hand. Of course, it was only one person's opinion, but just hearing that one means that the one I had before isn't all that there is, and that there are more out there. Nothing is simple and one-sided. You can't take what is given to you and accept it as fact without seeing it yourself, or without talking to people, learning things yourself.

No better illustration of your final premise than this entire entry. In fact, all the points you raise in these last two sentences are often cited to students before their journey abroad. They do not, however, mean anything in the abstract. These points need to be fleshed out—actualized—as you have done so effectively in your writing.

November 9 (Still in Vienna)

Yesterday was Mozart day—after breakfast (chocolate muesli, nutella, rolls, cheese, ham, etc.) we went to the Mozart house, where he wrote "The Marriage of Figaro." I was rather unimpressed by the set-up, but we bought a very informative little book for 40 shillings.

Then we went to Karlskirche (Karl's church), which was very

different from the other churches
we've seen (Stephensdom, Votir, St.
Peters). It was more marble than
stone, with really beautiful art-
work. The altar was <u>stunning</u>—it
inspired even <u>me</u> to pray.

After Karlskirche we came back to
the good ol' Anatol Hotel and took
a long nap/reading break. We had
Greek for dinner—Restaurant Levan-
tine—then took the subway and buses
to the Volksoper.

The opera—the actual singing and
music—was wonderful. You should see
how these people dress, though.
Ugh. And at intermission all the
little girls crowded around the
coatcheck guy (quite possibly the
only decent looking man in all of
Vienna). It was a rather adorable—
if pathetic—sight, all of them
wearing their best dress and their
mother's perfume.

I didn't think the direction of
the opera was at all good. All of
the action took place in one corner
of the stage for the entire first
act. Most of it took place there
for the rest of the opera as well.
Of course this would have to be the
corner of the stage I couldn't <u>see</u>,
but oh well.

And the <u>set</u>! Sets exist to <u>add</u>
something to a performance. If they
do not <u>add</u> something, they should
at least not <u>detract</u>. This set
detracted. It was atrociously ugly—
enough to distract my attention
from the music, the real focus,
after all, and I rather resented
this. In case you can't tell.

Sarah's last two entries (November 7-9) are from her trip to
Vienna during her semester break. We have included them,
even though they do not directly relate to the main themes of
this book. She was not required to make notebook entries
during her vacation. However, it is clear that the notebook has
become an important part of Sarah's intercultural experience;

she wants to write for all the right reasons: as a means for self-expression, as a tool for remembering, as a place to bring the diverse activities of her life into some kind of comprehensible whole.

November 11 (Back in Stockholm)

I cannot even begin to express how good it is to be back in this country. I mean, Vienna was wonderful, but the same thing happened coming back to Sweden this time was coming back from Berlin (that sentence doesn't exactly work, but I think you get the idea). As soon as I was back on Swedish ground, I was immediately filled with a sense of relief, of "it's so nice to be back!"

It's really comforting to feel that "homecoming" feeling here. I think everyone needs that sense of belonging and security, and it makes me happy that I feel it here. It makes me wonder when it began, and I think the answer is: when we got back from Berlin.

For the first time, I really felt that I belonged here when we landed in Malmo. I took a picture out the train window, and now have it prominently displayed on my wall. The air was Swedish, the water was Swedish, the signs were in Swedish—after feeling like such a foreigner in Berlin, I felt familiar with things again—I was on my own turf. It was great to feel that way about Sweden.

And that's how I felt yesterday. As soon as the plane touched the ground—Swedish ground—I didn't feel like such an outsider anymore. At least I know the subway system without an obnoxious tourist map. I can read a menu, I can buy what I need with a minimum of embarrassment.

It is interesting when you feel at home in a foreign land; it feels as if it occurred "suddenly," doesn't it? But actually, you've earned this sense of belonging. Of course it's almost time for the reverse to occur: going back to the States. Interestingly, for some students that "return" to one's native home is more difficult than the initial culture shock experience itself. Perhaps this entry is a preview of what you can expect to feel in the coming weeks.

I'm actually starting to feel at
home here. It's not the same feeling I have when I'm <u>really</u> at home
in the U.S. It's more of an awareness of not <u>really</u> being home, but
feeling comfortable anyway.

The best measure of your adjustment and integration in your
new country is when you begin to feel "at home." You may
wonder, like Sarah, when it happened. It is not a sudden development, because cultural assimilation is a process; everyday
you need to think less and less about culture as you become
more familiar with it. The culture which initially confronted you
as an alien and undefined entity suddenly becomes part of your
taken-for-granted understanding of everyday life. You know
you have grasped the underpinnings of a culture when you
stop thinking about it.

November 21

All of a sudden I'm going home for
Christmas. It's a very odd feeling.
I have been planning—since last
year—to be in Sweden until July or
so. I didn't plan to see my family
or friends for around 11 months.
My mom and grandma were going to
come here for Christmas, but now my
grandma is sick and her doctor
doesn't want her to travel. So
instead I'm going to go home. Home.
It even sounds kind of weird to me.
The strangest part about the whole
thing is that part of me doesn't
want to go. I definitely want to
see my grandparents—who are all
sick, unbelievably enough—, to
drive a car, to spend <u>dollars</u> and
<u>cents</u>, to rent movies, to <u>go</u> to
movies (dollar movies, here I
come!), to see my friends, to sleep
in my own bed.
But I also want to see a Swedish
Christmas. I want to stay here and
use the language I've been trying
to learn, instead of forgetting it

in Kansas City. I've been so set on
staying here, that now it's difficult to readjust my thoughts.
    I'm upset that my grandmother
can't come. She has been <u>so</u> excited
about coming here ever since I
started <u>thinking</u> about applying.
She's 82 years old—she's not going
to have <u>that</u> many opportunities to
come here again. But hopefully
she'll be able to come in the
spring.
    So now I'm starting to think of
all the things I want to do at home
(eat bagels, for example—<u>salt</u>
bagels with veggie cream cheese),
and I'm glad I'm going I guess. It
will be interesting to see how I
react to everything. Will home seem
different? Will I remember how to
drive? Will I remember how to open
a milk carton? Will I convert
everything to crowns? Will I turn
all the faucets the wrong way and
forget how to use door knobs? Will
I pull up on the toilet handle?
    Most of all, though, I guess I'm
glad I'm going home because I want
to share all the experiences I've
had this semester with my friends
and family before they fade in my
memory. There are <u>so</u> many things to
tell everyone about. And you can't
write it all in letters—it just
doesn't come through the way it
should.

Here we have another indication of Sarah's cultural adjustment. Compare her frame of mind in this entry, when she writes
about going home for Christmas, with her mood on Halloween
(October 31 entry).

November 22
    The first thing that struck me
about the hockey game last night
was how slanted everything was

towards the blue team. They were
all shown on the monitor, someone
was interviewed, they emerged on
the ice in darkness to be all the
more impressive when the lights
went on—it was like a <u>show</u>.

I thought—"Wow—this wouldn't happen in the U.S.!"

Then I hit myself and remembered
the first soccer game I went to. It
was 50 times more of a show than
this hockey game was. For a while I
was under the delusion that other
sports in America don't have that
one-team slant. Just soccer. Wrong.

So I started to think about the
baseball games I've been to. The
organ doesn't play for the <u>opposing</u>
team—unless maybe someone hits a
home run. The same kind of slant
exists—I imagine—in all sports.

I guess that's part of the
fun—instead of watching two teams
play a game, it's much more fun
when one is the hero and one is the
enemy. It's easy to create and foster this feeling with the whole
"show" attitude.

It worked on <u>me</u>—I rooted for the
blue team (even before they were
ahead 10-2). The main reason was
the little show before the
game—their team members were
presented as real people. The
uniform was just a cover. But the
yellow team was just a bunch of
masks.

The organized fan clubs were
interesting, too. (But where were
the cages? I was disappointed!)
It's such an odd concept to me. I'm
really not sure I understand it. I
mean, you can root for the team
whether or not you're in the fan
club—why join? But I guess it has
to do with the whole "being-a-part-
of-something" thing. The spirit of
the group would make the game more
fun—if the team does well. What do
they do when the team loses? Go off

a cliff like a mad pack of lemmings? A bunch of depressed people together can be a bad thing—perhaps that's where all of the fights come in. People who would <u>never</u> hit another person on their own, could do it if they feel that they have the sanction of the group. I guess that's the downside of a group mentality—it doesn't always work toward the best end.

November 26

Well, my research for the simulation (a class research project) showed me more than just child care and parent leave. The woman we interviewed at the day care center in Gorskarbacken, Bibi Fremoelig, also told us some things about herself that I found interesting. First of all, she has a 28-year-old son and two younger children, and second, she has a sambo (a live-in boyfriend).

Now I know I've written about this particular institution before —or I think I have—but I'm writing again because it really does impress me. Or maybe this woman just impressed me. She's got to be at <u>least</u> in her mid-forties, and she looked no older than 35. She lives with a man I'm assuming she's been with for many years—most <u>marriages</u> don't last that long—and she has two (or three, I don't remember which) grandchildren. Her son—the one with the kids—also has a sambo. So clearly he had a good experience with his parents' relationship if he's willing to do the same thing.

Perhaps this goes back to Wolf (an author read in class)—wasn't he the one who moaned about the breakdown of the family? I mean <u>clearly</u> the family isn't breaking down as much

Concerning your discussion of family values, this might be worth thinking about some more in a research format. Your comments are provocative comparing married to nonmarried relationships, but your social analysis might be better served with a closer, more detailed treatment.

as he seems to believe. The fact
that people choose to have a sambo
rather than be married only means
that it's the commitment, the relationship, that's important, and <u>not</u>
the marriage papers or the
ceremony. I think this shows a
<u>strengthening</u> of family values. The
last time I saw Bibi she was on her
way to meet her sambo, and the two
of them were going to go baby-sit
for their grandchildren. Certainly
this shows the strong family bonds
that exist in their family—not a
breakdown of anything, despite the
fact that neither of the two
couples (Bibi and her sambo, the
son and his sambo) are married.

This entry epitomizes the goal of an analytical notebook. Here Sarah integrates what she has learned from the classroom with her own cultural observations and experiences. Sarah has moved away from descriptive writing, and has clearly adopted an interpretive voice.

November 30

I cannot believe the simulation is
over. All year it has been
something that was <u>so</u> far away—it
signified THE END to me. And now
it's over. Where did the time go?
    The best thing about it, though,
is not what I learned about my <u>own</u>
focus, but what I learned from all
of the <u>other</u> groups. <u>And</u> the perspectives I got from you and Steve
(a professor who participated in
the simulation). There were times
when I was rather bored and
fidgety, I will admit, but even
then I really felt like I was
getting a lot out of it.
    It also hit me that I really have
learned a lot this semester. I
mean—I had a teacher who always
used to say this—"you have to <u>bring</u>

something to the party!" I felt
that I knew enough about what each
group was saying (maybe not economy
or foreign policy, but everything
else) to understand them, to
develop my own critique, and to
understand the critiques that you
and Steve gave. I felt I had
brought something to the party, and
even though the dialogue was going
on in front of me, there was also
enough in my head to have a
monologue going on there as well.

It will be nice to go home at
Christmas and know what I'm talking
about when people ask me about
Sweden. I may not be able to quote
statistics on anything but family
policy, but I'll have something
intelligent to say. The best thing
about that, I think, is that all of
the knowledge didn't come from one
class—or even four—but from being
here, and from all the students on
the program through the simulation.
I really hope other people had
similar experiences—I know many
did.

December 8

My last journal entry. There's
really too much to say.

I had six rolls of film developed
a couple of weeks ago—pictures of
my room that I sent to my friends
at school, pictures of the campus,
of Grona Lund when we went to the
last day of the season, pictures
from Berlin, Halloween, Vienna
. . . 36 X 6 (216) pictures, 216
images to bring the past four
months to life again, right there
before my eyes. They are wonderful
to have, but I don't know that I
need them.

When I was in Lund on the way
back from Berlin, I saw my own
boyfriend from when I was here

three years ago. We had the most
wonderful two months of our lives
together. It was the summer, I was
in a foreign land, and we were
insanely happy. When I saw him, we
relived every memory. For four
hours we went back and forth with
"Do you remember this?" "Do you
remember that?" "What
about. . . .?" He showed me his
photo album from that summer. When
he closed the album, he looked up
and said to me: "But I really don't
need the pictures. I have it all in
my mind. I can see everything, just
like it was yesterday."

So could I. I still can, and will
always be able to see every moment
of that summer in my mind as
clearly as if it was on a movie
screen before my very eyes.

That's the way I feel about this
semester. I love my pictures
because they do bring back
wonderful moments. But I don't need
them. Everything is preserved very
clearly in my mind. I remember the
first time I saw Laura. I remember
the pants Jennifer was wearing in
Newark—why? I remember when Chris
carried my enormously heavy bag for
me in the Castle Hotel and that the
first restaurant where we ate in
Sweden was Italian. I remember the
walking tour and your mood curve
speech. I remember dying of embarrassment when you surprised me—
shocked me—on my birthday (thank
you Carina) and the restaurant, and
46 people I didn't know sang "Happy
Birthday" to me. I was sitting with
Carl, Travis, Laura, Jim C., and
Stephanie.

I remember being so tired the
first three weeks I thought I was
going to drop, and the first time I
used a Bankomat (ATM) by myself. I
remember following Erin around
helplessly the first two weeks
because she could understand

everything and I couldn't
understand a thing.

If I went on like this I could run
out the ink on this pen and six
others, but you get the idea. What
I'm getting at here is that this
has been an experience that I will
always carry with me as clearly as
if it were yesterday. Some things
may fade, but I truly believe the
bulk will remain.

On my closets, I have been taping
up memorabilia (tickets to plays,
my first subway ticket, etc.) from
each month since I have been here.
Just looking at it I am <u>flooded</u>
with memories. 1 1/2 doors are full
from top to bottom, packed with the
things I have done, the places I
have been, the memories I have
collected. By the end of my time
here, these things will be covering
my closet doors—a whole wall of
little and big experiences
compressed into little remem-
brances. But when I take them down
next summer, the memories will
remain.

I came to Sweden—and on this program—for a lot of reasons. I <u>loved</u>
Sweden when I was here before. My
two months here were the happiest
time of my life. No one deserves to
be as happy as I was in those two
months. My family is Swedish on my
mother's side. My grandmother
(whose father emigrated from
Småland to Minnesota in the 1870s)
was <u>so</u> happy that I chose to go to
Sweden—there is nothing I could
have done to make her happier
(except maybe make her a great-
grandmother before she dies!).

I chose <u>this</u> program because I
wanted to go to school in a city
(Williamstown just doesn't count),
because the classes looked great,
and because of the trips to Berlin
and Budapest. In none of these
things have I been disappointed. I

guess I kind of said this in my
entry on the simulation, but I have
learned <u>so</u> much this semester.

The best things I have learned,
though, are not about Sweden,
really, but about myself. I have,
quite accidentally, developed
political opinions since I got
here, something I never had much of
before. My view of Sweden has
opened my eyes to the United States
and allowed me to see what I think
are the flaws in my own country. I
have more faith in my own self-
worth.

I have made such wonderful
friends. I was so afraid, last summer, that I wouldn't like anyone,
or that no one would like <u>me</u>.
Instead I have friends who I know
will last a lifetime. I am very
picky about my closest friends, and
that type of friendship is not
something I take lightly. To know
that I have friends like that from
this semester would have made it
worthwhile even if the semester had
been terrible otherwise. But it
wasn't. Instead, we had a great
time <u>together</u>. I guess what I'm
saying is—you have great people
applying for this program, and that
reflects on the type of program it
is. I think it's <u>very</u> special.

Researching Culture:
Writing for an Academic Audience

In the previous chapter, Sarah presented several notebook entries that prompted us to comment on the potential for enlarging the scope and depth of her ideas. On several occasions we asked her to consider elaboration: could Sarah envision using these spontaneous observations and theoretical insights as starting points for more writing? In this book, we have concerned ourselves with writing as a means for cultural discovery and understanding. To now, we have stressed the value of the analytical notebook as an opportunity to write informally, speculating and experimenting with initial insights and observations. But even as we encouraged you to use the notebook as a place for recording the often digressive and undeveloped material of daily life in a foreign culture, we also discussed the importance of harnessing these diverse impressions into a coherent intellectual or theoretical framework. For example, when Sarah wrote about her visit to the Marabou chocolate factory, she wondered, "How is it possible to keep a factory clean?" She also made several comments about the industrial-labor relationships observed in her tour of this chocolate factory. The entries were some of her best—filled with careful observations and thoughts. However, as we asked after each of them, could she develop her thinking further by connecting what she observed at Marabou to what she has read about labor relations in Sweden, or perhaps learned about the subject in classroom lectures?

The analytical notebook is a wellspring for trying out ideas, but it is also the place for beginning more formal academic writing, such as for a term paper or a final examination. As we discussed in chapter two, analytical writing brings together elements of both expressive and transactional prose. When it is time to begin preparation for an exam or to search for a paper topic, it is wise to re-read your notebook. In doing so, you will discover the issues and themes that have been consistently interesting to you as a writer over time; a sustained level of personal involvement is always a worthwhile starting place for formal research. On the other hand, you may simply stumble across a rich topic in a single entry. Sarah might well have centered a research paper on her experiences at Marabou; the initial generalizations she conceived in observing labor at the plant itself—e.g., the way in which work was conducted, even the link between worker attitude and the quality of the product itself—are potential topics for research. These topics, in turn, suggest other ones: What was the philosophy that underscored the particular labor design Sarah noted in place at the factory, and why was it instituted? Does Marabou conform to representative labor models in Sweden? Or is it an aberration? Do the policies of the factory reflect certain employer-employee relationships that are unique to Sweden, or is it possible to see similar attitudes in other countries? Sarah probably could not answer questions such as these by herself. She would first need to go to the library, interview employees and management at the factory, perhaps consult with her professor(s). This is research, and it obviously pushes Sarah beyond the scope of her initial notebook entry. But if she chose to record in that same notebook the additional information that would accrue as she worked her way through these various sources, the analytical notebook's importance would deepen accordingly.

We are confident that, like Sarah, if students re-read their analytical notebooks when they are ready to begin thinking about a research topic, they will also find observations and tentative generalizations which need to be tested by more formal study.

There is something unique about the intercultural experience which will tempt you to want to make quick generalizations about your new society and culture. Culture shock is so disorienting precisely because it questions your own generalizations about social life. There is, consequently, a tendency among study abroad students in the midst of culture shock to over-generalize, that is, to infer broad truths from early experiences. For instance, you may observe that your host family in France is patriarchal. Based on this first impression, you may be inclined to conclude that the French family must be patriarchal. This generalization may indeed turn out to be true, but you cannot make such an inference based on your observations about *one* French family. You need to test your own personal observation by conducting a more systematic study of family life in France. This research would help you discover whether your host family is typical or idiosyncratic.

As we discussed in chapter one, students suffering from culture shock have a natural desire to bring conceptual order as soon as possible to their shattered frame of reference. Nobody likes thinking that he or she is clueless about prevailing cultural practices. Moreover, the sooner you feel capable of trusting that your own observations and impressions are accurate, the better position you will be in to understand your new culture. The research process, then, is an integral part of cultural adjustment and assimilation. Before you can accept any generalizations as true, you need to make sure that they are rooted in solid evidence—that their truth is not just restricted to you alone. Your analytical notebook is a potential resource for identifying what warrants further empirical investigation.

The Analytical Notebook and the Research Process

Several years ago, one of our students, Jeanne, was required to keep an analytical notebook for her last class in Nursing, a senior clinical experience where she was actively engaged on a cardiac recovery unit. Although asked to perform many of the same tasks required of hospital staff, Jeanne was still a student, and consequently her notebook entries highlighted her unique transitional status. As a final project for this course in clinical nursing, Jeanne was additionally required to produce a research paper on some aspect of the nursing profession. In one of her earliest notebook entries, reproduced below, Jeanne expressed an interest in discovering ways for encouraging patients to maintain a post-operative routine of diet, sleep, exercise, etc.

When she first began to think about this topic—in class discussion with other nursing students and her professor—Jeanne had no idea how to go about researching it. But as you will see in the course of reviewing several other entries from her analytical notebook, as Jeanne continued to record her floor nursing experiences, the daily events she chose to write about eventually provided the necessary direction.

> Tuesday, April 14
> We're in a circle. So how's clinical? How's clinical?! My mind races. I want out of this. I'm tired, frustrated, lost in the middle of where I should be. Where I am. Are you all finding that you're really getting adjusted to your floors? Adjusted. Adjusted to what? An inconsistent environment with vague expectations. Alone. Tired with sore feet. Giving everything to this program—what's left for me?
>
> So how are your papers coming along? Jeanne, do you want to share with the group?
>
> How can I write a theory paper when I can't even face the library? I just want to sleep. Avoid. Sure, I'm interested in what determines whether or not a patient will comply w/a prescribed regimen. Basically what can we as nurses do to increase patient compliance through our care?
>
> A good idea they tell me. An idea, yes. But how am I going to handle it? Good intentions, but where's the motivation for the action??

Several days later, Jeanne wrote another entry that recorded her impressions of co-workers and the professional world they inhabit (and she was about to join). Although this entry would appear to shed little direct insight into the research topic we see referenced above, commenting instead upon the stressful occupation of a hospital staff nurse, in the last paragraph Jeanne begins to circle back to issues of nursing care and the importance of assessing patients as individuals. Near the end of the entry, Jeanne asks, how important is the personal relationship between nurse and patient in terms of influencing what the latter will learn about his illness and the need for modifying behavior? This question—perhaps unintentionally, but such associations happen when you put your thoughts into writing—becomes particularly relevant to what the rest of the entry is about: If nurses are centered on accomplishing the physical tasks that need to be performed on the floor, how can they possibly find either the time or energy to establish the kind of interpersonal contact with patients "necessary to build and develop a relationship"?

Friday, April 24
At clinical today I just watched the nurses. They are all so task-oriented. Their pride seems to stem from their ability to get their work done: meds given, baths done, beds changed. Racing through the day—no time to think about what I should have done an hour ago.

Hell bent on tasks. Where's the humanness in these ladies? Who are they?

The traditional female
got married
raised a child
decided to become a nurse
got a divorce
bitter
frustrated
and bringing their problems to work.

Just like me.
They seem so callous. Fail to pick up on lead-ins by the patient expressing feelings about himself. His illness. These interactions are necessary—to build and develop a relationship. How can they teach if they don't know the patient? Neglect his maleness? Who takes the time to assess the learner? Where is HE coming from? What has any of this got to do with my report?

At this point in her writing and observing, Jeanne is not at all sure how any of these insights relate to her research report. But after several more entries, where Jeanne continued to speculate about the interpersonal relationships between floor staff and patients, she participated in a notable experience working directly with a patient and his family. Not only does the tone of this writing differ markedly from Jeanne's earlier entries, suggesting the level of excitement she gains from her active role as nurse-teacher, it also records what would become an impressionable interaction between a supportive wife and her recuperating husband:

Friday, May 8
Mrs. Reed walks with Mr. Reed down the hall. She reminds him to take his pulse. She squeezes his hand. She washes his anti-embolytic stockings. She is full of questions about activity. Diet. Such a relief to find someone ready to learn. I teach all afternoon. I love it! Absolutely love

it. I feel so very close to these people. I feel that I've really made a difference in their lives. I feel confident around them.

Mrs. Reed has read the entire information booklet, inside out. Their
daughter and husband come and visit from California. I talk to them in
the staff lounge: What are their concerns, their fears, their feelings?
What's going to be difficult for them?

A day like today can make up for weeks of frustration.

At various points in her notebook, Jeanne reminds herself
about the research report she fears she is avoiding. But because
she has been dutifully writing down various observations about
the floor—e.g., nurse/patient behavior, interactions between
patient and spouse—she is in the position to re-read her
thoughts and connect them, again through the act of writing. As
she does so, random reflections about daily life as a nurse on the
cardiac unit provide the opportunity for Jeanne to advance her
research thesis. Maybe the process of teaching a patient self-
knowledge about his illness, she begins to formulate in her next
entry, is not the exclusive responsibility of the nurse. In fact, as
her interaction with the Reeds has taught her, if the nurse opens
this domain to include a patient's family—especially the
spouse—the clinical nurse's educational efforts may be more
likely to extend beyond the patient's stay in the hospital.

The following entry documents the importance of Jeanne's
deliberate re-reading of earlier entries; these earlier writings, in
turn, stimulated Jeanne's thinking forward, motivating her to
forge a writing connection with her research thesis. The act of
cognitive synthesis is a mysterious process, but Jeanne's experience would suggest again that writing is a primary vehicle for
encouraging the mind to create such important affiliations. As
David Huddle reminds us in *The Writing Habit*: "In both memory and imagination, one thing leads to another. The most
important decisions and discoveries in my own writing have
occurred between one sentence and the next, between one paragraph and the next. The whole force of what we call 'creativity'
may in fact be just the process of one thing leading to another,
the energy of the imagination, the energy of memory" (19).
Huddle's definition of "creativity," while defined in terms of
mental and emotional growth, is finally only possible through a

physical act: the labor of getting language down on paper. In her notebook's final entry, Jeanne illustrates this very point:

> Friday, May 15
> Got to go on my hunches. I just reviewed my entries about theory. I have been asking so what will make it stick? What will make him comply? Change behavior, day-by-day, night-by-night—follow the regimen (entry 4/14).
> As I reread my entries about the Reeds I have an idea. I need to research but just how important is the spouse? Surely by getting through to Mrs. Reed and motivating her, I was actually motivating her husband (entry 5/8). If nurses direct their teachings at the spouse in the presence of the patient will this increase compliance? The cardiac rehabilitation lit suggests that programs have been successful in providing information. However, these prescribed behavior modifications are frequently neglected after the patient returns home.
> I feel confident about Mr. Reed's discharge. Why? Could it be that I feel Mrs. Reed will take over from me? Carrying over my role as supporter, advocate, teacher. That I've planted a <u>seed</u>?
> What about the nurses? I am surprised on how harsh I hit on them in earlier entries. Still they talk of men in disgust. The nurse could relate to the spouse. Direct her teaching/information at her. Develop a trust. Nurses are human. Maybe they just need the right listeners?

As you might conclude from the preceding entry, Jeanne went on to compose a formal paper entitled: "The Role of the Spouse: The Nurse-Family Relationship in Cardiac Rehabilitation Care." As she acknowledges above, she needed to go back to the library and read what scholars in the field had already published about post-operative compliance training programs. But now she could be particularly attentive to what this research revealed—or failed to reveal—about the role of the family in a post-operative regimen. In the actual writing of her research paper, Jeanne still continued to rely heavily upon her analytical notebook. Her own record of working with the Reeds became a case study that Jeanne used to illustrate the research she had unearthed.

Conducting Research

This last entry from Jeanne's notebook represents a good illustration of the point where personal observation and interest intersect with information that must be found through particular research sources and institutions. For many young writers there is a tendency to think of research as simply the accumulation of what's out there (data) and then the organization of that material into a coherent report that summarizes what these sources say. This perspective on research ignores the personal dimension: what you are interested in finding out about a particular subject, and how other writers have contributed to the collective knowledge about this topic. Jeanne needed to "test" her clinical speculations regarding the potential role of the spouse/nuclear family in post-operative care against what professionals in her field had already published about this subject. But the scholarship written in this area of specialization would have meant less to Jeanne if she had come to it without the inspiration of her own experience and her own writing. Similarly, without the initial written observations made by Sarah while visiting the Marabou factory, the subsequent list of "research questions" we raise in the beginning of this chapter would be devoid of a real-life context, and, therefore, less interesting and less passionate—for Sarah as well as her potential readers. The point is, that for both Jeanne and Sarah, formal research originated from personal interest and writing; it is a discourse that should begin with personal observations and speculations, but eventually evolve beyond the limits of the known, beyond the limits of the self.

Good research is never passive. It always involves an active process of questioning, pursuing, evaluating, and revising your thinking as you learn more about the subject. What you eventually learn depends upon how you are changed through what you come to know.

1. *Find a question/issue that interests you.* Re-read your analytical notebook carefully. Look for recurring topics that have stimulated multiple entries. Has your professor pointed to potential areas of research in written comments to your notebook, as we did in the last chapter with Sarah's? Unconsciously, Sarah posed several rich topics throughout her notebook; discussing them with her professors and classmates would have made her more aware of their research potential.

2. *Information sources are everywhere.* Research is not only a matter of finding data in books and articles; it involves all sorts of human interaction. Depending upon your research topic, this may include such empirical methods as interviews with people who have information on your topic, such as surveys which tap the opinion or attitude of a relevant population. For example, Sarah would have learned a great deal more about Marabou if she were to interview one of its laborers. In addition, consulting with the library staff is always helpful. Even if you feel confident in moving about electronic databases in your particular institution, most of these databases do not go back very far, and some of them may be difficult to access. If you share your research with members of the library staff, their expertise will most often save you time and energy; they will point you in directions you never would have considered by yourself.

3. *All research is strategic.* As a researcher begins to accumulate information from outside sources, it is never enough simply to record these data. Good research always connects the information you assemble from outside sources with your own knowledge about the subject. Again, note the potential role of analytical writing here: As you consider the information available from different sources, *evaluate* what these sources are saying. Perhaps begin by summarizing their positions, but always conclude with an evaluation. Write about how a scholar either contributes or fails to contribute to *your* research thesis. What is the author's particular point of view—and how does this bias confirm or disagree with your own (or other writers') assessment of the information? In other words, use your notebook as an interactive tool—a place where the knowledge you have learned from others truly becomes your own. Repeatedly reconsider the scope of your topic—is it too narrow or broad?—and is it worthwhile adjusting your thesis in light of the information you are uncovering?

Too many students, graduate and undergraduate alike, make the mistake of believing that they can't possibly begin actually writing until they have done enough research. However, delaying the writing process accumulates notecards and source citations to the point at which you may feel overwhelmed by the sheer amount of material amassed; when it becomes time to assemble this work into written form, the idea of where to begin or how to structure it all poses a terrifying reality. This approach is a sure recipe for writer's block. Instead, always make your own writing an intregal part of collecting research.

After viewing Hieronymus Bosch's famous painting, *The Garden of Earthly Delights,* in the Prado museum, located in Madrid, Spain, Michael, a third-year abroad student studying at the University of Madrid, decided to write an interpretative research paper analyzing Bosch's attitude toward sin as it is reflected within this particular work of art. He reviewed several scholarly books and articles in the library, and soon discovered that most art historians believe that Bosch meant this painting to be an allegorical representation of The Fall from Grace—a moral lesson in which lascivious behavior leads to an eternity in hell. Most of the scholars Michael researched tended to agree with Ludwig von Baldass, that "There can be no doubt that, for all Bosch's profound pessimism, he was not only a pious Christian but also an absolute orthodox Catholic" (76).

As Michael continued his research, however, he felt that the critics were offering a perspective that didn't quite account for what he got from the painting. Here's what he wrote in his notebook after several days in the library:

> I'm not really sure how much I agree with what the authors [of schol-arly texts] argue. Gibson, Beagle, von Baldass, et al. believe that H.B. was so obviously in opposition to the Garden portion of this painting. I'm still not so sure that anyone who understood the attraction of human sin—flirtation, sexuality, and pleasure—as sensuously as Bosch portrays could possibly feel so TOTALLY against it. I know I'm not seeing this from the perspective of a medievalist, but the Hell panel of this painting is simply the opposite of the Garden panel, isn't it? The two merely reflect two opposing principles.

Michael finds himself at an interesting crossroad. He's done his research, but in the process has ended up questioning and even disagreeing with the sources he's read. This debate poses the opportunity for Michael to show his reader that he has thought long and hard about what the scholars say about the work under discussion, but that after doing so he wishes to argue a varying position. Michael might want to revise some of the language he employs in the above entry, making it more appropriate for a research paper, but the concepts represented could easily become the crux of a formal interpretative essay. He would want, perhaps, to acknowledge that he is interpreting Bosch's work from his own twentieth-century perspective, and to account for how this would produce a response that might digress from existing scholarship. But teachers like to see students engage in similar acts of academic discourse. Michael is surely taking a risk when he challenges the published authorities of the field, but he appears to be doing so with a sense of critical balance; his notebook entry indicates that he is prepared to support his thesis with interpretative evidence.

4. *Clarity emerges through multiple drafts.* Clarity of argument comes not from having a perfect idea of what you want to say to begin with, but rather from reworking what you have written into a form that is clear and convincing. This never happens in the first draft. The formal quality of a piece of writing is largely invisible as you struggle with it initially. Only in retrospect, after you have something down on paper, is it possible to sit back and ask yourself: is this what I wanted to say? Later in this chapter we will have more discussion about the importance of adhering to a thesis—or central argument—in any kind of academic writing. But the task of maintaining such consistency is especially crucial in research writing.

Usually so much material is being presented that the writer must strive to exert control over it, providing a clear purpose or design that unifies the various elements of the report. Strive to announce your thesis early on. As you continue to write, keep that assertion always in mind, elaborating on it, documenting it, qualifying it, but always coming back, directly or indirectly, to the purpose of your writing—the key concept that holds all the parts together. Even if you demonstrate an overwhelming command of the research data, the manner in which this material is connected—how it all makes sense—remains the single most important aspect of research writing.

If you have been writing in your analytical notebook throughout the process of accumulating research, practicing the methods of critical evaluation mentioned earlier, you are establishing a "bridge" between the information you have discovered from other sources and your own sense of how it all fits together. If the analytical notebook is employed at the center of this process, as Michael demonstrates in his work on the Bosch painting, the writer may be able to establish important points of transition from the notebook to a formal paper. Thus, the analytical notebook is not only a font for discovering early research ideas, it is also a place for joining personal writing to scholarship.

5. *Revising Research.* As we've mentioned above, revision is an essential part of research writing. You may have conscientiously worked on each section of the research paper, but until you read it as a whole, you can't judge the degree to which it conveys a clear, coherent message and represents a logical integration of material. As you read your document from start to finish, you'll probably discover that information is missing, incomplete, or inconsistent with the thesis of your paper. Consider the following steps:

— read the whole document, checking for continuity and coherence. Do its parts conform to your stated thesis?
— focus on whether all parts of the research are accurate, documented wherever appropriate, and complete;
— is the writing organized? Would sub-headings help the reader follow the presentation of ideas?
— does the introduction create a certain level of interest with a highly visual example or narrative anecdote appropriate to the subject of the writing that follows?
— does the conclusion actually conclude? Rather than merely summarizing the contents of the paper, does the ending suggest something further about the implications of your research, thereby leaving the reader challenged and still thinking?
— finally, consider the details of style: word choice, punctuation, and other elements of grammar that add clarity and precision to individual paragraphs and sentences;
— get away from the written document for a while before you complete its revisions—this will help you take a fresh look at it, as your readers will ultimately do;

— ask a couple of classmates or friends to read it over. This peer review is so helpful that many instructors require it as part of the assignment. Remember that the kind of feedback someone can provide will depend upon the state of your research. If the draft is rough, the feedback will be general; if the draft is more refined, the feedback can be more specific.

Examining the Essay Examination

What does a well-written essay have to do with cultural understanding? Actually, quite a lot. If the writing process is also a mode of learning, then the more you develop your abilities to use language—making it analytical, focused on a thesis—the more you will know about your subject. Put simply, the more you write, the more you learn. But the reverse is also true: the more you learn the better position you are in to write well. The relationship between learning and the writing process is therefore dialectical, that is to say, mutually reinforcing.

Essay examinations continue to be a major testing component of coursework in universities around the world. This is particularly true in western Europe, where most classes end with some sort of written examination. In a very real way, you begin to prepare for this exam on the first day of class, as you notice your professor's assignments, biases, and perspectives. Since essays are usually written for an audience of one—your teacher—what you say on an exam might be viewed as an intellectual dialogue with a person you know quite well. This doesn't mean that your writing should get chummy or collo-quial—in fact, strive to produce analytical rather than expressive writing. In forming your ideas on paper, be aware of your professor's perspective. If you intend to present an opinion that will run contrary to your teacher's, be prepared to back it up especially well. In other words, feel free to express your opinion in the answer you construct, but also pay attention to your instructor's position and clearly acknowledge it somewhere in the essay. Then go ahead and strike out on your own. There is probably nothing more boring for an instructor to read than thirty attempts to recapitulate her lectures. Strive for a reasonable balance here: use the information you have learned from lectures and textbooks, but bring in your own awareness of what is important about this material, how it relates to the exam question as well as the way in which you interpret it.

The key to performing well on an essay examination is to understand completely what the questions are asking. The language of a given assignment will often contain hidden clues which reveal directions toward composing a potential answer. Consider, for example, this examination question from a recent American literature midterm:

> The general tone of Crevecoeur's *Letters of An American Farmer* presents an image of America that finds restatement in the work of Emerson and the transcendentalists: It is that of a young, beautiful, optimistic, and enduring country which is destined to complete the cycle of history begun in Europe. Compare this version of America to that found in Mark Twain's *Huckleberry Finn*.

First, notice how much information is already supplied in the topic itself: an implied chronology, that Emerson and the transcendentalists are coming out of an American literary tradition that was shaped by earlier writers such as Crevecoeur. Moreover, the exam also supplies you with a solid definition of what Crevecoeur and the transcendentalists generally felt about America. Lastly, the topic also suggests that this version of America must be compared or contrasted with Twain's perception. These are your starting points, and perhaps the easiest way to begin composing a response would be to assemble evidence from *Huckleberry Finn* that either agrees or disagrees with the Crevecoeur-transcendentalist position.

However, it is quite possible to argue that Twain's novel presents at the same time *both* a negative portrait of America's social institutions and a positive example of American individualism in the survivalist instincts of Huck. Another way to answer this question, then, would be to refrain from making the distinction regarding whether *Huck Finn* is essentially an optimistic or pessimistic work, but instead to demonstrate where the novel both disagrees and concurs with the perspective associated with Crevecoeur and the transcendentalists. The word "compare" in the exam question allows you this flexibility.

The term "comparison" usually means a larger, more inclusive approach to the topic that may include both similarities and differences. But if you were asked instead to *contrast* Twain's book with these earlier writers, you would want to emphasize the differences only. Therefore, any question that asks you to compare or contrast may be requesting

1. the differences between two or more things
2. the similarities between generally dissimilar things
3. an explanation of one thing in relation to something else
4. a basis for evaluation and/or argument.

All comparisons and contrasts require you to go beyond individual positions, theses, or texts—to think about the *interrelationships* between characteristics of two or more concepts. Such essays demand writing that is analytical—interpretive and reflective of your own voice—as opposed to being merely descriptive. Thus, your analytical notebook, with its emphasis on establishing connections between different aspects of everyday life, is a good place for practicing the comparisons and contrasts often requested in essay writing.

If an essay examination does not request some type of a comparison or contrast between individual concepts, it will generally ask you to analyze a single problem or circumstance, or some aspect of it:

Discuss the importance of several key historical events that gave rise to World War II.

What is the significance of Orlick's relationship to Pip in Dickens's *Great Expectations*?

Both questions ask you to explain the relationship between parts and a larger whole. By first identifying and then explaining the significance of the individual components—considering what, when, where, why, and how they operate—we gain a fuller appreciation of how these unique elements work together to produce a deeper comprehension of the whole. To understand Orlick's connection to Pip, for instance, you must first establish that Orlick is a reflection of one dimension of Pip's larger personality—the latter's dark alter ego. It is really quite unnecessary to delve into the "other sides" of Pip's complex character to answer this question; in fact, pursuing them may distract your reader from the real purpose of the writing and thus weaken your analysis. The exam requests only information about where Pip and Orlick share mutual correspondences, and this should remain the focus of your entire essay.

Preparation for an Essay Examination

A few days before the exam is distributed (or scheduled in class), spend a couple of hours marking passages in texts and your analytical notebook that you consider significant. Try to anticipate if not the questions you will be asked, at least the subject matter most likely to be covered. This activity will accomplish two things. First, it will refresh your memory by helping you to refocus material studied weeks ago. Second, these recollections will get you thinking about the most important aspects of the work under discussion. Instead of beginning the exam on the day you receive it, your preparation will place relevant information at your fingertips, giving you an obvious head start on assembling evidence. This process is especially valuable prior to in-class open-book examinations. Premarked notations and quotes will save you precious minutes during the exam itself.

As we discussed in the earlier section of this chapter dealing with research, your analytical notebook is also an excellent source to begin studying for an essay examination. Before taking an exam or writing a given essay assignment, read through your notebook entries on areas germane to the examination topic(s). As with research writing, sometimes you may discover whole sections or passages that require only slight modification for inclusion into the essay. Aside from generating ideas to use in composing a response, the notebook is also the place to begin the actual writing of the essay itself. In the case of a take-home exam, use your notebook to freewrite about the exam topic. The notebook will not only help to start the flow of writing itself, but a couple of good entries may become the basis for your essay.

Structuring Essay Answers

Once you understand the type of information the exam question requests, you should plan a response to it. First, make a simple list of main ideas. This basic outline will generate new concepts and simultaneously help in formulating the language you will need to construct a coherent argument. Second, use a written plan to keep your writing focused on the subject. After you have composed such a plan, check it against the examination request. Are the topics you intend to discuss relevant to what is being asked?

In an essay exam, many students tend to write without a sufficiently developed focus or thesis. Often, their writing merely summarizes events or lists information. Students who have not practiced analytical writing consistently find it difficult to present their own voice or perspective and to construct arguments that interpret the natural world, the concepts of a text, or social reality. By simply saying as much as they can about a particular topic or text, they trust that the torrent of information will duly impress the teacher or somehow manage to strike upon a response relevant to the question. Consider, for example, the following essay written by a history student in response to a question asking him to compare Hitler's politics to Gandhi's:

> I have chosen this question because each man is so unique, and the personalities of both serve as studies in contrast.
>
> Both men held unimaginable powers over their followers. The difference is the way in which each man chose to use it. Hitler brainwashed his people, redirecting their collective anger toward the Jewish population, so that he could focus his attention on conquering the world.
>
> Gandhi used his powers not for personal advantage, but instead to unite his people as one. Hindus and Muslims were to be united so that they might defeat the British through non-violence and civil disobedience. A good example of this was when Gandhi and his followers marched towards the beaches and began making salt illegally. In response, the government made thousands of arrests and set up a blockade of soldiers to stop them. The beating Gandhi's followers

received from the troops was passively accepted in the hope that the soldiers would re-evaluate their moral priorities.

On the other hand, Hitler abused and tortured his enemies, just for the sake of killing them. He created death camps, such as Auschwitz in Poland, where thousands of people were devalued and murdered.

Even though the personalities and goals of these men were completely different, their followers felt they represented hope and a better future life. In the case of Hitler especially, he promised to restore the German honor that had been usurped by the Allies after WWI. Gandhi promised to unite India as a whole and free nation—one that could also be proud of itself after years of humiliation from the British.

Both of these men were considered as heroes by their followers. One of them committed inhuman acts; the other fought for the freedom of his country and won it, without shedding a drop of human blood.

What has this student done right in this answer? First, he seems aware of the need to create a comparison between these two historical figures, and to do so, he must mention information about both. Thus, he tries, in the examples of Gandhi's salt-making encounter and Hitler's concentration camps, to muster evidence to support his generalized statements about each leader.

What are the problems in this essay? Most glaringly, perhaps, this writer has failed to create a *close* comparison between the two men. The comparisons he does summon are not developed clearly enough, and there are too many occasions where a reader loses sight of the purpose behind his writing. Moreover, his emphasis is exclusively centered upon differences, as if the writer would not dare to suggest that there might be points of similarity between Gandhi and Hitler. Obviously these men were uniquely different personalities, but constructing a comparison that brought together possible ways of making a connection—e.g., that both were capable of and willing to manipulate others for the sake of their respective causes, that both men did indeed end up shedding many "drops of human blood" in fighting their respective causes—would serve to create a critical balance to accompany the contrasts being made.

In discussing strategies for structuring essay exams, several of our colleagues suggested that the strongest part of any essay should be its beginning. Since professors read dozens of essays in a rush, students should give them what they want up front, and certainly within the first paragraph. The standard advice in structuring essays is to create some version of a "funnel" shape: Start broadly by stating and defining the most important elements, or thesis, of your argument. Then, gradually narrow or specify your main argument through examples and illustrations of the points raised initially in the thesis statement. In this way, your examples and analyses will refer to concepts you have established, and your supporting evidence can be tailored to fit the major points which began the essay. This principle can be illustrated in the paragraphs that follow, taken from a midterm examination in which Susan was asked to relate the theme of Walt Whitman's short poem *"A noiseless patient spider"* to his larger poetic vision:

> Walt Whitman was a poet who wrote about the unity of all things. He took Emerson's doctrines to their extremes, believing that not only were the diverse and individual elements of the universe related to one another but, in fact, that they were reflective of the same identical thing.
>
> Whitman's themes were about everything—a blade of grass, a prostitute, a dying man alone on a battlefield—and he believed sincerely that no one thing was better, or worse, than another. A spider (which before this class I would probably squash) is only a small part of the "whole," yet is still connected to the "whole," just as one human being is representative of a larger humanity.
>
> The spider is isolated, as are those individual men and women who fail to explore and learn from their surroundings and others, but the difference is that the spider creates a web that "connects" things together. Whitman's verse accomplishes the same sort of connecting. He unifies everything and everybody in poetic song. In the first half of Song of Myself, the poet takes all of life's experiences and makes them his own—he observes and studies them—and then seeks to understand how they are connected to one another.
>
> In "A noiseless patient spider," he asks his soul the same question: "Where do I stand? / Surrounded, detached, seeking spheres to connect them." Only by "connecting" himself to everything and everyone he observes can the poet, like the spider's web, "form a bridge" that will link him to the rest of the world.

In the opening paragraph, Susan begins her analysis with a broad assessment of Whitman's poetry; she even includes a mention of Emerson's influence on his work. After establishing the unity theme in Whitman's poetry, she ends her first paragraph by tying this concept to *"A noiseless, patient spider"*: "A spider (which before this class I would probably squash) is only a small part of the 'whole', just as one human being is representative of a larger humanity."

In the second paragraph, Susan's analysis becomes more specific, centering on the relationship between the metaphor of the spider's web and Whitman's broader poetic principles. This represents the heart of the exam answer—its closest effort at responding to the instructor's question—and because of this should be expanded beyond the argument Susan raises. But what she does argue in this paragraph is what the teacher of this exam is looking for in evaluating her writing: the ability to make explicit the connection between Whitman's spider and other poems.

The use of the "funnel" structure as an organizing metaphor in this essay aids Susan in developing her argument in a systematic and coherent manner. As the answer unfolds, she gradually narrows her analysis from the general to the specific, so that by the conclusion Whitman's poetic vision and the symbolic spider web become synonymous in purpose: "Only by 'connecting' himself to everything and everyone he observes can the poet, like the spider's web, 'form the bridge' that will link him to the rest of the world."

A well-written essay—whether composed during a timed in-class examination or in response to a take-home assignment—reflects the strengths described in this chapter. It is organized and focused; it demonstrates the ability to analyze and/or engage comparative thought; it shows the capacity to assemble and assess information; and it indicates an understanding of course material and the capability to shape this understanding into writing appropriate to the exam topic. The take-home essay is closely related to its in-class brethren in form, content, and purpose. However, since they are each composed under different circumstances, there are some slight variations in their manner of production. Primarily, a take-home examination affords the chance to edit, to revise, and to rethink what you have composed, while the in-class examination is essentially a single draft freewriting exercise. Further, the take-home exam provides the opportunity to incorporate research—class notes, quotations from texts, the analytical notebook, and sometimes published scholarship—directly into the composition. Be sure to employ the checklist provided at the end of the "Conducting Research" section of this chapter (pp. 118-119); many of the same revising and editing concerns we raise about research writing are also appropriate to constructing essay examination answers.

6

Cultural Change and
Personal Discovery

We have argued in this book that the mission of intercultural education ought to be cultural adjustment and integration. Toward that end, we have shown how writing about your own everyday cultural experiences is an effective way of overcoming culture shock and of eventually understanding and deepening an appreciation for your new culture. In this, our final chapter, we will discuss the ways in which writing can be seen as part of a general philosophy of how best to integrate into your new society. This philosophy is most accurately defined in terms of self-empowerment.

The most effective way of adjusting to a new society is to try things on your own; you should always attempt to do things for yourself. Your first inclination will be to turn to your program's staff for help in finding solutions to the many problems which surface regarding daily life in a new society. Your program staff will certainly provide you with information, guidance, and support. But it will be your own experience of trial and error that will help you best to discover and understand your new culture. Thus, the mission of intercultural education should be to promote cultural integration by imparting to students the knowledge necessary to act independently in a new society.

From the Culture of Narcissism to Personal Autonomy

The challenge of feeling autonomous and acting independently in your new society is difficult not only because you do not know the culture, but also due to the fact that many American students are *coming from* a culture of narcissism. Allow us to explain briefly this culture of narcissism.

There has been much written about the narcissistic patterns of contemporary American culture (Lasch 31) and how Americans feel disconnected from a larger community (Bellah 1, passim). Briefly, the culture of narcissism is characterized by individuals who have lost their sense of community and who, as the term "narcissist" denotes, are primarily self-concerned. This self-preoccupation, however, is not motivated by self-regard, but, rather, self-doubt. Thus, contemporary narcissism is very different from the "rugged" forms of individualism associated with the American past. The causes for this self-doubt in contemporary society are multi-faceted. Lasch and others have pointed to the ways in which consumer culture, the "helping" professions, and bureaucratic authority have undermined a sense of confidence and competence among many Americans (154). Lacking the power and/or information to make decisions for themselves, many Americans have become dependent on others—whom the former deem to be "experts"—to make "rational and efficient" decisions for them.

The concern with the self is also fostered by a discontent with society. More specifically, the accurate recognition that American institutions are in trouble—the schools are failing to teach, the family is breaking down, the streets are no longer safe, politics is often defined by special interests—leads to social cynicism and nihilism. Discontent with society, coupled with the conviction that it cannot change, forces the individual to turn inward for a refuge. In other words, legitimate social criticism can atrophy into narcissism. The perceived failure of politics results in many individuals believing that personal survival is the only realistic goal. With little hope for a better society such individuals find it difficult to meet the social obligations of citizenship or to make the political commitments necessary to alter the social conditions of their lives.

In fact, social obligations appear to the cynic and nihilist as foolish. If you do not think that anyone is playing "by the rules," the norms and traditions associated with citizenship become a game for fools. In such a narcissistic culture, the normative underpinnings of community break down and a preoccupation with the self becomes the dominant way of coping with social discontent. The narcissistic illusion is that you can survive and find fulfillment by escaping the necessary, albeit difficult, challenge of building a better society. In other words, individuals want a better life without recognizing that the attainment of this goal requires an improved society. Such individuals, therefore, unfairly demand more from themselves at the same time as they expect less from their society. This ideology is doomed to fail because it only reinforces personal frustration and a narcissistic culture's general spirit of apathy.

We should add that the self-doubt we have been discussing is often masked by an arrogant outward demeanor. In the classroom, such students are quick to confront all forms of authority, as exemplified by their attitude towards their teacher or an author they have been assigned to read (Wagner 297). This disregard for authority reflects a contempt for anyone capable of uncovering the narcissist's underlying insecurity and self-doubt.

We have presented this brief overview of a narcissistic culture because its influence leaves students (or anyone) poorly prepared to confront the challenges of cultural adjustment and integration which require:

a)   a sense of adventure;
b)   a propensity for risk-taking;
c)   an acceptance of your limitations;
d)   an ability to laugh at yourself;
e)   a willingness to learn by trial and error.

All the above personal attributes presuppose a relatively autonomous and confident person who is not afraid of failure. Now we are not suggesting that all, or even most, students are so narcissistic that they cannot adopt these important characteristics. But we do believe that most American students in some ways are affected by the dominant cultural patterns of their time. At the minimum, this means that many American students begin their study abroad experience feeling, in varying degrees, cynical about society (politics) and insecure about their ability to find success (no matter how it is defined). Certainly, the degree to which you may feel insecure as you enter your new country reflects also your youth and an accurate recognition that you are about to face a real challenge.

Students who may feel cynical and insecure about life and themselves sometimes discover that the intercultural experience can, in the end, be a powerful antidote. As we have discussed throughout this book, you will find yourself in social situations which will demand that you confront any fear of failure. The reality of culture shock is that it makes us all feel like children; lacking a social compass, we tend to feel lost a lot of the time.

The study abroad experience can provide a sort of shock therapy for individuals coming from a narcissistic culture who also lack personal confidence and direction. It forces you to engage in a process of both cultural discovery and self-definition. The process of writing is itself an act of self-consciousness as it allows you to understand better your new culture and yourself. In this way, writing becomes a facilitator for both cultural discovery and self-definition.

In earlier chapters, we have demonstrated how writing leads to cultural discovery, struggle, and assimilation. Let us now turn to examples from students' analytical notebooks which illustrate how writing, understood as an act of self-consciousness, fosters self-definition.

How Do Study Abroad Students Change?

Intercultural educators often speak and write about how much students change as a result of living abroad. Students themselves also are conscious that they are not the same persons before their trip. But it isn't always clear how they have changed. Students who write analytically about their intercultural experience are more self-conscious about their life abroad, appreciative of the ways in which they have changed. We will now address this issue by looking at three interrelated areas in which our students have identified such change: self-definition, politics, and personal style. In addition, this chapter will discuss the ways in which gender differences affect how students react to the intercultural experience. Lastly, we will conclude with a discussion of culture shock in reverse, or what happens when your intercultural experience ends and you must go home.

It sounds like a cliché to report that students "grow up" while studying and living abroad, but they do. Most students mature because they must learn to adjust to their new culture. The experience of culture shock encourages students to adopt certain personality traits associated with adulthood. In terms of personal growth or student self-definition, we have observed that our students believe they have changed because they have learned to see the world from a different perspective. Listen to Crista at the end of her semester reflect on how she has "grown" personally and how she has assimilated culturally.

> I am American in body and mind, but now I feel a bit of Swedish has gotten under my skin. I feel a part of this culture right now and I think some of that will stay with me for the rest of my life. I will never see things as I saw them before. I feel that I have grown as a person . . .
>
> After reading my notebook over again, I've realized how much I have changed. I have to laugh at some of my entries, especially when I complain about people pushing my back on the subway to make me move.
>
> I hated it because I felt it was an invasion of my personal space. But now I can't remember the last time someone did that to me. I guess I've stopped noticing it.
>
> When I read about all the places I have been to and the things I have done, I'm pretty proud of myself. I've been super motivated to learn, learn, learn. And I hope I get more chances to learn and experience more about life.

We explained earlier how the intercultural experience creates a new paradigm or perspective on the world. You literally come to see things differently or see things that you were oblivious to before. Note how self-conscious Crista is about how she "will never see things like I saw them before." Crista remembers, for example, how she complained in some of her early entries about the fact that she was being pushed on the subway. But at the end of her semester, she writes: "But now I can't remember the last time someone did that to me. I guess I've stopped noticing it." This recognition is noteworthy, for it signifies that Crista is no longer conscious of a cultural difference; like the Swedes, she simply doesn't notice it. In this way, she now has more in common with the Swedes than the self who arrived months ago. Lastly, we would like to emphasize Crista's emerging level of self-confidence—"I'm pretty proud of myself" —born out of successfully completing one of the toughest tests of her life.

Barbara reflects on a similar changed perspective:

> Perhaps that is the biggest thing that's changed for me in my four months in Sweden. I think I have learned to see things as Swedes see them, to understand their values and their concerns. My first few entries seem to be about individual experiences, whereas my latest entries are more concerned with Swedish ideas and issues. I really feel that I'm much better at identifying with Swedes now. I still don't feel that I'm Swedish, but I don't feel that I'm in a foreign country.

The development of a new vision appears to lead many students to develop a more tolerant perspective towards cultural differences. As Barbara suggests, as students come to see the world from the perspective of their new culture, they begin to stop feeling like "foreigners." The experience of seeing things with "new eyes" can lead to greater cultural empathy. As we explained in chapter one, students in the midst of culture shock often react angrily towards perceived cultural differences. But at the end of their stay abroad, these same students often learn to appreciate the differences, or literally stop seeing them as different.

It is also important to point out Barbara's observation that her early entries were more about "individual experiences, whereas my latest entries are more concerned with Swedish ideas and issues." This change in focus reflects a move from expressive writing (personal reactions, observations, etc.) to analytical writing where she is attempting to interpret political ideas and cultural patterns.

Seeing the world differently—from the perspective of another culture—does not mean that you lose the perspective of your own society. It means that the paradigm through which you see and interpret the world is now more multi-faceted. The capacity to see and understand everyday life from multiple perspectives brings maturity and sophistication to the ways in which you react to, and make judgments about, social life. More specifically, such cultural empathy tends to mitigate against seeing the world in "black and white." Your perspective allows you to discover the "shades of gray" in arguments about culture and politics. Consequently, your own position on issues begins to be more nuanced as it reflects a greater awareness of, and empathy with, the perspectives of others.

Here is clear evidence of how the intercultural experience serves as an antidote to a narcissistic culture: the capacity to empathize with others stands in opposition to narcissism. Such a capacity reflects individuals whose confidence enables them to question their own perspective because they have come to respect the perspectives of others.

In this way, we witness the relationship between personal growth and politics. Living and studying abroad is inherently a political act. The very fact that students discover cultural variation allows them to demystify their own culture. Recognizing that their own traditions and customs are not natural, monolithic, or necessarily the best, allows them to consider the value inherent in other customs and traditions. When you return home, you will probably continue to debate the merits and liabilities about <u>both</u> your cultures. But consider the potential for growth in this debate alone: you are now in a position to compare your native culture with a foreign one, and this engaging activity will make you more conscious (if not appreciative) of both. We will come back to the experience of returning home in the last section of this chapter. But for now, let's continue our discussion of how students change.

The argument above does not imply that all or even most students become "political" or that they become political in a particular manner. We mean "political" in the broadest sense of the term: becoming more aware of the world outside. The discovery of different cultures, along with the recognition that there is a larger world "out there," forces many students to become interested in political issues. Thus, the emergence of any interest in the purpose of politics—social change—is another example of a retreat from the common student refrain that also is reflective of a narcissistic culture: namely, that politics are irrelevant in a world that cannot change. This statement may sound melodramatic, but we believe that when students witness both cultural differences and the ways in which they themselves change, it becomes possible to imagine that politics can make a difference. For example, listen to Betsy:

> As a government major, I have become more and more interested in policy areas than I used to be. I've seen here how public policy <u>can</u> be affected by the people and how important participation is. I'm not so anti-government as I used to be.

The legitimation of the political process can be seen as a consequence of students discovering cultural variation. We are not suggesting that all such variation can be explained by prevailing political differences; that is, if we only changed the politics all countries would have similar cultural patterns.

Culture is, of course, a more complex reality also shaped by history, religion, and language. But we are arguing that the intercultural experience forces students to focus on things *apart* from themselves—on other peoples and their ways of life.

Another example of such a cultural focus can be found in students who, for the first time, discover "the arts" during their time abroad. Art, film, and theater provide students with a dramatic lens through which they discover what is unique about their new culture and what it shares with their native culture.

What You Wear and What You Eat

We have so far in this chapter emphasized how students develop the ability to see the world from a different perspective. Students who have adopted another lens also change their behavior.

Students' behavior begins to change at roughly the same point that they see everyday life from the perspective of the native population. Why? As soon as students "see" how things are different, there is a natural tendency—from a sociological and psychological point of view—to want to conform to the behavior of the people from their host country. All human beings need to feel that they "fit in" in some way to the social system in which they find themselves. For a study abroad student who is experiencing culture shock, this urge can be intense. The desire to conform is also reinforced by an evolving respect for the prevailing culture. Consequently, emulation of your culture's customs and traditions should be seen as a positive step towards cultural integration and adjustment.

At the same time as we are advocating a "when in Rome do as the Romans do philosophy," we are not suggesting that you must agree with, or in fact follow, every cultural practice. There will remain particular cultural patterns or traditions with which you feel personally uncomfortable. For example, in Scandinavia many families take family saunas together in their own homes. Students living in such families are often invited to share the cultural practice. Clearly, many American students would find this ritual uncomfortable, and it is appropriate to indicate your feelings in no uncertain terms. But our larger point here is that when there is no instance of a difference in values, you should do whatever you can to connect to the culture in which you are living. Thus, we cannot overemphasize the importance of trying new things, of challenging yourself by broadening your cultural perspective.

Some initial behavior changes are highly personal and most evident in terms of cultural "style." By style we are referring to such things as hairstyle and how students dress. One of the first things students themselves recognize very early after arrival is that they "look different." This feeling is reinforced by their perception that the natives are looking at them "funny."

Around the world American students are often stereotyped as dressing a certain way. And, of course, American students (men in particular) often arrive in their new culture looking like the typical American student: wearing sweatshirts, ripped jeans, and in the case of men—a baseball hat. You will certainly discover that such an American "style" may be becoming more popular in your new society. But when this style is exhibited in conjunction with other American cultural practices such as speaking English—often loudly from the perspective of the natives—the consequence is that attention is called to yourself as "foreign."

The longer you feel foreign the longer you will experience culture shock. Thus, it is not an act of patriotic betrayal if you want to start looking like the majority of people you now see every day. This is, of course, the underlying psychology of fashion; people want to be accepted by those they define as "cool" or who have the power to define you as an "insider" or "outsider." Not surprisingly, the natives of any society have this power.

Therefore, the tendency for students to change their haircut and style of dress can be seen as natural and positive. But such symbolic changes are certainly **not** a prerequisite for, or a definition of, cultural adjustment and integration. Students who decide not to change their outward style or demeanor may be equally or more "in tune" with the native population regarding cultural values, norms, or other customs and traditions.

Another change in student behavior often involves eating habits and preferences. Many students report that their experience abroad broadens their appetites to a whole variety of food. For example, students may discover that cheese is eaten in the morning or perhaps in the evening, everybody seems to eat fresh bread, dinner may not be served until nine at night, and that the coffee is stronger. Moreover, American students soon recognize that how they use a knife and fork (or in some cultures using such utensils at all) is considered "strange" by everyone else. As you read about these examples, from hairstyle to how a fork is held, please remember that individually these may appear to be trivial issues. But taken together, they are part of what will define your initial cultural awkwardness. As we have argued throughout this book, culture shock is the realization that you do not understand the unwritten rules of everyday life.

Other new rules of everyday life that students discover and that may be different from their own include: the frequency of shaking hands or kissing each cheek upon greeting another person; how loudly or quietly individuals talk in public; how often people touch each other in public and use hand gestures for emphasis; how people meet and "court" each other; how strangers are greeted or not greeted in public places; and how to answer the telephone by informing the caller of your identity and doing the same when calling yourself. This is not meant to be an exhaustive list, but, rather, a sample of the often unspoken and unwritten rules or customs which students over time begin to emulate. Some students may alter their behavior out of respect for the indigenous culture and a consequent desire to fit in, while others may be inspired to change simply because they enjoy partaking in a new cultural practice.

In fact, these are the kinds of customs, norms, and traditions which students tend to adopt as the reality of culture shock recedes. A good indication of cultural adjustment is the experience of having friends or family come to visit you and observing their behavior from the perspective of the native population. For example, as we discussed earlier, Swedes tend to speak more quietly than Americans in public places. Our students often find themselves in public with their American friends and family trying to get them to temper their voices. They often report to us that they are "embarrassed" by such "American behavior."

Intercultural educators are often asked if students change their values while living abroad. On this issue, we are not prepared to make an empirical claim. First of all, a change in values, compared to the rules of everyday life cited above, is difficult to observe. The behavior of students over time, as opposed to what students say they believe, is the best measure of a shift in values. Certainly, it is significant if students themselves think they have changed. But actual behavior is a more accurate measurement.

The issue of whether students change their values is a topic which warrants more systematic research. We have no doubt that the intercultural experience forces students to question their own values, as the various voices cited from the student notebooks demonstrate, and that many students do in fact alter both their political and personal values. But how many, and the degree to which these students actually change their values and corresponding behavior, are questions which require a longitudinal—tracking student beliefs and behavior over time—study.

Gender Differences

In the spirit of posing questions that require further systematic study, we would like to raise the issue of understanding gender differences in assessing how students perceive and understand cultural differences. It is significant to point out that 63% of all American students who study abroad are women (Institute of

Internatinal Education 90). There are many suggested explana-
tions for this phenomenon. One is that women tend to major in
disciplines—the humanities—in which their professors are
more supportive of study abroad. Second, studies suggest that
women are socialized to define themselves in terms of their *relations with others* (as opposed to men who tend define themselves
in terms of their *separation from others*) (Gilligan 1, passim). This
difference may provide another reason why women are more
likely to be interested in the experience of forging intercultural
relationships.

What we have observed in our own students' analytical notebooks supports Gilligan's thesis. Women are much more likely
to write about how they discovered cultural differences *in the
context* of their relationships with individuals from the indigenous culture. In this way, women tend to be very adroit at recognizing the social aspects of their personal encounters. Men,
on the other hand, tend to write more abstractly about culture:
how norms and traditions are different from their own. Thus, as
teachers, we often find ourselves encouraging men to write
about the ways in which their everyday experiences reveal different cultural norms and traditions. This is not to imply that
women are always better writers or adjust more easily to a new
culture. But in this particular case, where the challenge of the
analytical notebook is to connect personal experiences with the
prevailing culture, the social reality of gender differences may
give women a certain advantage.

We raise these issues briefly in order to sensitize men and
women to how gender differences *may* affect how they understand and write about their intercultural experiences. If it is
true, as we have consistently argued, that cultural discovery
leads to personal discovery, then the writing process may help
students become more self-conscious about how gender affects
the ways in which they see and interpret cultural differences.
We would like to suggest that when students read each other's
notebooks as advised in chapter three, they include at least one
notebook from a student from the opposite sex as a way of
"checking" to see if indeed gender appears to be affecting how
they are writing about their intercultural experiences.

We now turn our attention to another form of culture shock. We are referring to going home and re-experiencing your own culture with "new" eyes. The re-entry process can be difficult because you will find yourself in familiar social situations—at home with your family, or at school with your friends—and discover that your reactions to certain events or circumstances may differ from friends and family members making you feel like a "stranger" in your own country. This is the experience of culture shock in reverse.

The Process of Re-Entry: Culture Shock in Reverse

Since you probably have not yet discovered the reality of culture shock, you may be skeptical about the concept of experiencing culture shock in reverse. In fact, however, most students do experience a necessary re-adjustment to their native culture. Most, in turn, reacquaint themselves with their native culture. This reacculturation is necessary because most students eventually adjust to their new culture.

We have suggested that an accurate barometer for measuring cultural adjustment is when you stop thinking about cultural differences or about culture in general. Sometime near the end of your first semester you will recognize that what consumed your attention for so long—culture—is now something you take for granted. At precisely this point, your new culture has started to become habitual, part of your own frame of reference. You no longer have to think about culture because what was so foreign has now become "natural." This degree of cultural assimilation makes you vulnerable to experiencing culture shock when you re-enter your own society. Because this additional culture shock is unexpected—returning home to things you missed and know so well—it can be that much more unnerving.

This experience should not be over-dramatized as almost all students certainly do re-adjust to their own culture rather quickly. Nevertheless, it is shock to feel disoriented in your own country. The culture shock which occurs upon returning home is not a result of students consciously bringing their new culture home. You may not realize how well you have adjusted—how much of your new culture you have "picked up"—until you come home and encounter contrasting cultural experiences. You will confront familiar customs, traditions, and other cultural patterns which you may now find uncomfortable or to your disliking. Clearly, you will also re-discover certain American customs which you will be quite pleased to embrace as your own. Thus, for a short period of time you may find yourself in cultural limbo; that is, not being sure which culture fits you best.

This last intercultural challenge is perhaps the clearest illustration of how cultural discovery leads to personal discovery and self-definition. The result of living in a different culture presents you the opportunity to make a new set of personal judgments regarding values, beliefs, sense of style, and other social preferences. Such decision-making requires both introspection and self-knowledge. Therefore, we encourage you to continue writing in your analytical notebook about your everyday cultural experiences when you return home. As when you were facing a foreign culture, writing about how you experience your native culture will bring clarity and meaning to your thoughts and feelings. Moreover, writing can help provide distance and perspective to your study abroad experience. It is a cliché, but also a truism, that intercultural students often cannot assess their overall experience abroad until they distance themselves from the experience. Such distance is created by simply traveling home and by the process (discipline) of writing.

Writing offers students the opportunity to establish a necessary separation between emotions and thoughts. The process of writing forces you to name and define your emotions, and, thus, to think clearly about what they mean. In this way, writing allows you to simultaneously stand back from how you think and feel, while at the same time, creating the necessary precondition for getting closer to the truth about your thoughts and emotions. Writing "freezes" emotions and thoughts thereby enabling the writer to examine them with a certain degree of objectivity, or distance.

Your notebook will prove valuable not only as a tool for making meaning out of complex thoughts and emotions, but, also, as a way of recording fresh observations of American culture gleaned from a new perspective. Typical of such observations are:

1) "Everything is so big, from the food portions to the size of the cars."
2) "I can't get used to the crime. Why do people accept this?"
3) "Nobody realizes there is a whole world out there."
4) "The pace of life is too quick."
5) "Everything that is public property here is so run down, from the parks to the public transportation system."
6) "How come people don't take time out for coffee and conversation?"

It is common for returning students to make such critical observations as a result of reverse culture shock. There certainly will be times when you will be glad to be home because of particular American customs and traditions. But "coming home" can still produce a certain degree of disorientation. Thus, students feeling this unique version of culture shock will lash out at Americans for the same reasons they initially "bashed" the culture of the country in which they studied.

The "struggle" of coming home is expressed by Andrea, returning from a year of study in Copenhagen:

It is hard to remember the struggle and the tears of loneliness and frustration. Looking back, I remember only the fun and good times. The early difficulties remain only in my journal. For me, the real struggle was coming home. To be in Copenhagen early one afternoon and Burlington, Vermont, that same evening was excruciatingly disorienting . . .

In another entry from Andrea, her disorientation is further explained:

I feel so foreign to life here (in the States). Everything appears the same, the same people working in the supermarket, the same buying the groceries. But I am different. I have left a part of me in Denmark . . . Everything here is big and inefficient—the toilets, houses, cars, packaging. I feel very much like an outsider, even among people I know. No one told me I would have more culture shock coming home. How could I have culture shock? This was my home. But it happened.

It is important to note here that Andrea's frustrations origi-
nate from everyday life experience—"the toilets, houses, cars,
packaging"—in America. Similar to the experience of culture
shock abroad, the feeling of disorientation at home results from
recognizing that the old routines or rules of daily life are now
perceived as "strange." Experiencing your own culture as different, however, can be more disconcerting than your initial culture shock abroad. It is natural to feel like an outsider in a different culture; you may even expect it. But as Andrea points
out, it is worse to feel "like an outsider, even among people I
know." The alienation from those you know is a consequence of
recognizing that you are different from them. The "problem" is
not with them, however, but with you; you are the one who has
changed.

Feeling culture shock in your own country will make you
continue to ask yourself questions about your values, beliefs,
and which culture makes you feel the most at home. Chances
are the answers you come up with will reflect a synthesis of
what you admired about the culture discovered abroad with
what you believe is right or good about your native culture. Our
intent here is not to present the experience of culture shock in
reverse as a problem, but, rather, as a very important facet of
the complete intercultural challenge. The experience is not over
when you get on that plane to come home. Only when you
return home to discover that you now see old routines with
new eyes will you be in a position to perceive how dramatically
you have changed. You are different now because you have
assimilated aspects of the culture you have geographically, but
not psychologically, left behind.

This process of cultural comparison and self-examination
promotes personal growth and maturity. We explained in chapters one and three how culture is experienced unconsciously by
most individuals. After your return home, you will have the
capacity—to a certain degree—to stand apart from both cultures, viewing them consciously and critically. Such a bi-cul-
tural perspective can be emancipating because it empowers you
to make certain cultural and political choices about how you
want to live. You will then understand that culture is not a universal reality, but instead exists in many different forms.

Clearly, all cultures have things in common because human beings share certain limitations imposed upon them by nature. However, awareness of cultural diversity makes students realize that no one culture has a copyright on what is best. Moreover, having the ability to recognize culture's effect on individuals—including yourself—places you in a position to limit its influence, and, thereby, to enhance your personal autonomy.

Students discover that they return as different people from the ones they were before journeying abroad. Coming home may be disorienting, but you will soon re-adjust and begin to recognize your own growth and maturity. There is a wonderful sense of satisfaction among most returning study abroad students. They know they have met a terrific challenge. Listen to Jennifer reflect on how her intercultural experience reminds her of sailing across the ocean:

> They are both like sailing. There are stormy days when you're thrown around a bit, you don't understand and you wish you could just click your heels and go home. But there are also those magical moments when the dolphins seek you out and ask you to play, the sun shines, and the auto pilot is working so you can relax and don't have to think as hard about what you are doing or saying. Everyday routines, things you used to take for granted, become a chore; asking for the milk, using the toilet. The food isn't always what you want, or your favorite dish, but you make do. It's strange that you can get so used to living in this new method that it seems stranger still when you taste "normal" life again when you get together with other Americans. You learn a lot about yourself and about what's important to you and where you stand in the world. And you get a glimpse of how some people's lives are and how much is out there to do.
>
> I have challenged myself, frustrated myself, and satisfied myself. I have experienced life in another country, in another language, lost my personality, my being, and gained them back again.

In this thoughtful entry, Jennifer expresses a multitude of emotions that accompany cultural adjustment and self-discovery. It is interesting to note how Jennifer captures the ways in which returning home brings her "full circle." The initial culture shock shakes your cultural roots forcing you to lose your "personality" and your "being." The re-adjustment process brings you face-to-face with how you have changed, and in turn, you regain your sense of self. This sense of loss of self and its re-discovery may appear overstated, but we believe that such terminology is an accurate indication of how self-conscious you will become of how profoundly you will change.

Concluding Words

By the time you finish this book, you are either about to board your plane or you have concluded your orientation period abroad. Either way, we wish to close our book by reiterating our central arguments and commending you on your decision to study and live abroad.

At the end of your adventure in a new culture, we hope the written word proves as valuable and rewarding to you as it has to the students we have quoted in this book. If you were initially skeptical as to how writing was in any direct way relevant to your intercultural experience, we trust that our main point is now clear: writing about your everyday cultural experiences will help you discover and understand your new culture. Writing is much more than a means to reveal what you know; it is a creative tool which will lead you to discover knowledge and decipher its meaning. Far more interesting and accurate than your best pictures or postcards, your analytical notebook will provide you with a permanent portrait of your cultural trials and tribulations, as well as your personal triumphs and joys.

In this book, we have presented you with a discourse on culture shock and the writing process. Your own writing will represent your own discourse on what will most likely be both one of the most challenging and rewarding experiences of your life. You should feel proud that you had the wisdom to study abroad. Such a decision requires courage, a sense of adventure, and a strong sense of cultural curiosity. We hope that this book has helped you enhance your commitment to understanding your new country's unwritten rules of everyday life by writing them down.

Bon voyage, and don't forget to bring a pen.

Works Cited

Applebee, Arthur, et al. "Learning to Write in the Secondary School: How and Where." *English Journal* (1981): 78-82.

Arons, Arnold. "Teaching Science." *Scholars Who Teach—The Art of College Science Teaching.* Ed. Steven M. Cahn. Chicago: Nelson-Hall, 1978.

Bellah, Robert, et al. *Habits of the Heart—Individualism and Commitment in American Life.* New York: Harper and Row, 1985.

Britton, James. *The Development of Writing Abilities.* London: Macmillan Education, 1975.

Darwin, Charles. *The Red Notebooks of Charles Darwin.* Ithaca: Cornell UP, 1980.

Dostoevsky, Fyodor. *The Notebooks for Crime and Punishment.* Ed. and trans. by Edward Wasiolek. Chicago: Chicago UP, 1967.

Foucault, Michel. *The Order of Things,* 1966; New York: Pantheon Books, 1970.

Freire, Paulo. *The Pedagogy of the Oppressed.* Trans. by Myra Bergman Ramos, 1970; New York: Continuum, 1988.

Fulwiler, Toby. *College Writing.* Boston: Scott, Foresman and Company, 1988.

Gilligan, Carol. *In a Different Voice.* Cambridge: Harvard UP, 1982.

Heclo, Hugh and Henrick Madsen. *Policy and Politics in Sweden.* Philadelphia: Temple UP, 1987.

Huddle, David. *The Writing Habit: Essays.* Salt Lake City, Utah: Peregrine Smith Books, 1991.

Kuhn, Thomas. *The Structure of Scientific Revolutions.* Chicago: Chicago UP, 1962.

Lasch, Christopher. *The Culture of Narcissism.* New York: W.W. Norton and Company, 1978.

——. *The Minimal Self.* New York: W.W. Norton and Company, 1984.

Magistrale, Tony. *Stephen King: The Second Decade.* New York: Twayne, 1992.

Milner, Henry. *Sweden: Social Democracy in Practice.* Oxford: Oxford UP, 1990.

Open Doors, 92-93. New York: IIE (The Institute of International Education), 1993.

Rutherford, Ernest. *The Collected Papers of Lord Rutherford of Nelson.* New York: Interscience Publishers, INC., 1963.

Sandler, Karen. "Letting Them Write When They Can't Even Talk? Writing as Discovery in the Foreign Language Classroom." *The Journal Book.* Ed. Toby Fulwiler. Portsmouth, NH: Boynton-Cook/ Heinemann, 1987.

Strauss, Michael and Toby Fulwiler. "Writing to Learn in Large Lecture Classes." *Journal of College Science Teaching* 19 (Dec. 1989/Jan. 1990): 158-163.

Tilton, Tim. *The Political Theory of Swedish Social Democracy.* Oxford: Clarendon Press, 1990.

von Baldass, Ludwig. "Hieronymus Bosch." *Bosch in Perspective.* Ed. James Snyder. Englewood Cliffs, NJ: Prentice-Hall, 1973.

Wagner, Kenneth. "The Crisis in the American Classroom: Narcissism and Economic Decline." *Rinascita della Scuola* 9 (1985): 297-313.

Whorf, Benjamin Lee. *Language, Thought, and Reality*. Boston: MIT Press, 1956.

Wolfe, Alan. *Whose Keeper?* Berkeley: California UP, 1989.

Suggested Reading List

Berthoff, Ann. *Forming/Thinking/Writing: The Composing Imagination*. Rochelle Park, NJ: Hayden, 1978.

——. *The Making of Meaning*. Montclair, NJ: Boynton/Cook, 1981.

Emig, Janet. "Writing as a Mode of Learning." *College Composition and Communication* 28 (1977): 122-128.

Flower, Linda. *Problem-Solving Strategies for Writing*. New York: Harcourt Brace Jovanovich, 1989.

Fulwiler, Toby, ed. *The Journal Book*. Portsmouth, NH: Boynton-Cook/Heinemann, 1987.

Geertz, Clifford. "Thick Description: Toward and Interpretive Theory of Culture." *Contemporary Field Research*. Ed. Robert Emerson, Boston: Little, Brown, 1983.

Graesser, Arthur C. and Gordon H. Bower, eds. *Inferences and Text Comprehension*. New York: Academic Press, 1990.

Griffin, Williams C., ed. *Teaching Writing in All Disciplines*. San Francisco: Jossey-Bass, 1982.

Hess, David. "Teaching Ethnographic Writing: A Review Essay." *Anthropology and Education Quarterly* 20 (1989): 163-176.

Laubscher, Michael. *Encounters with Difference—Student Perceptions of the Role of Out-of-Class Experiences in Education Abroad*. Westport, CT: Greenwood Press, 1994.

Lewis, Tom and Robert Jungman, eds. *On Being Foreign—Culture Shock in Short Fiction*. Yarmouth, Maine: Intercultural Press, 1985.

Magistrale, Anthony, et al. "Writing Across the Technology Curriculum." *Issues in Writing* 3 (1991): 174-195.

Paige, Michael, ed. *Education for the Intercultural Experience.* Yarmouth, Maine: Intercultural Press, 1993.

Plain Talk about Learning and Writing Across the Curriculum. Virginia: Virginia Department of Education, 1987.

Prictchard-Evans, Edward, ed. *Peoples of the Earth.* Danbury, CT: Grolier, 1973.

Tate, Gary and Edward P. J. Corbett, eds. *The Writing Teacher's Sourcebook.* New York: Oxford UP, 1988.

Twain, Mark. *Innocents Abroad,* 1869; New York: NAL, 1966.

Tocqueville, Alexis de. *Democracy in America,* 1835; New York: NAL, 1956.

Turnbull, Colin M. *The Forest People.* New York: Simon and Schuster, 1973.

Index

Kenneth Wagner is the Executive Director of
The Swedish Program at Stockholm University.

Tony Magistrale is an Associate Professor in the English
Department at the University of Vermont.